Explori
Ancient \

George O

with additions by **Rodney Legg**
and photographs by **Tony Pritchard**

Adam and Eve

 Dorset Publishing Company, Knock-na-Cre, Milborne Port, Sherborne, Dorset DT9 5HJ

Publishing details. First published 1982. Main text
copyright George Osborn © 1982, with sections by
Rodney Legg headed ''Access Rights'' and ''Soil and
Cultivation'' in each site description and other additions
and captions being copyright Rodney Legg © 1982. Modern
photographs by Tony Pritchard were taken specially for
this work in March 1982 and are copyright Dorset
Publishing Company © 1982. Format and presentation
devised by Rodney Legg and copyright Dorset
Publishing Company © 1982.
Printing credits. Typeset by Clare Malling at The
Fosse Bureau, 36 Princes Street, Yeovil, Somerset.
Layout by Tony Pritchard at Creative Heads Studio,
Abbey Cottages, Montacute, Somerset. Printing, with
advice from Roger Toogood and Les Rivers, by Adams
and Sons (Printers) Limited, at Burcott Road,
Hereford. Trade sales distribution by Dorset Publishing
Company from Knock-na-cre, Milborne Port,
Sherborne, Dorset DT9 5HJ, telephone 0963 32583

International Standard Book Number
(ISBN) 0 902129 43 0

Contents

Preface

I have been encouraged to write this guide to the outstanding sites of antiquity in Wiltshire by the reception of my book on Ancient Dorset. This book proved very popular with the educated but non specialist public and according to the numerous letters of appreciation received gave much added pleasure to both holiday makers and residents of the county. In one case a gentleman in Dorset of 75 years of age wrote to thank me and to say that although he had lived all his life in Dorset he had no idea that the great hill-forts of Hod and Hambledon were only five miles from his house and he had never visited them until his attention was drawn to them by my book.

I have therefore ventured to write this book in the hope that it will encourage the people of Wiltshire, and that visitors to the county may also go and find for themselves, the remote and beautiful sites of antiquity which will give them much pleasure. It is not meant to be a text book for the learned but a simple guide with explanations for the general public.

Bearing in mind that many people will have come a long way to find these remote sites I have included short notes on other places well worth visiting in the neighbourhoods and also mentioned, wherever possible, where refreshments may be obtained.

I should like to acknowledge the great debt I owe to Rodney Legg who not only edited this book so thoroughly but also has helped in many ways with his enthusiasm, ideas and additions. I should also like to thank my secretary, Mrs. Joan Gosnold, who helped me so much during the long task of visiting and recording these ancient monuments. It only remains for the author to hope this book will enable readers to get as much pleasure, solace and contentment from visiting these lovely sites as he himself has done.

Introduction

It has often been said and with good reason that Dorset and Wiltshire contain more sites of interest archaeologically than all the rest of the British Isles put together. The reason for this is clear — all the great invasions from Europe came via the Dorset coast and then made their way through the Dorset Downs into the fertile hills and fields of Wiltshire. The reason why the invasions always came this way was that Kent, Sussex and Hampshire were covered by inpenetrable forests and swamps whilst in Dorset the chalk hills with only a thin cover of earth could not support many trees and in consequence the clear open dry downland made an ideal site for invasion and settlement. The chalk was comparatively easy to work with their primitive instruments such as antler picks.

Of course, one of the first questions the thinking man must ask himself when he sees a vast triple ring fort is who built these and how and when.

The answer to who made them goes right back to pre-historic times. Neolithic man, from 4,500 BC, built simple circles of earth to protect his family and cattle from attack by wandering bands of warriors. Within these simple walls they often had their homes, simple pit dwellings being the earliest known type in these lands. Examples can be found at All Cannings Cross, Swallowfield and Fifield Bavant. The inhabitants lived in well-like shafts about four to six feet deep; the sides were lined with straw and the tops covered with a thatched roof. Access was by means of ladders. Other pits in the neighbourhood were used for storage. From about 4000 BC up to 500 BC life appears to have altered very little. From this time onwards the scene changed rapidly with the continual migration of tribes driven out of France into England.

The first of these invaders, Iron Age A immigrants, brought with them a knowledge of fortress building already well advanced. One such group landing at Lulworth Cove rapidly threw up a linear earthwork of defence on Bindon Hill, the first beach head in England, and then, when established built the powerful fortress on nearby Flowers Barrow.

Soon, as tribe after tribe arrived, we find that, broadly speaking, each block of downland between two rivers was occupied by at least one hill fort and often by several. Some of these were lived in but for the most part they were places of refuge when invaders approached.

Most of the early Iron Age (A1 and A2) forts were of one ring with counterscarp outside their ditch. The entrances were frequently turned inwards to render invaders more vulnerable.

The ramparts were often timber revetted to prevent overspread into the berm and ditch. These Iron Age A hill forts were constructed between 450 and 250 BC, and the ramparts were rather slight in keeping with the purpose of enclosing cattle or to keep out marauders.

From 250 BC onward there were constant invasions from the continent and this led to the demand for stronger hill forts of Iron Age 2.

About 150 BC a further wave of invaders arrived amongst whom the most important were the Veneti from Brittany who were masters at sling-stone warfare. As they soon discovered the Chesil Beach they had an inexhaustible supply of pebbles to use as sling-stones. By 50 BC the Veneti had been driven out of Brittany by the Romans and were active in Wessex either adapting the early Iron Age forts or constructing new ones.

The principle these people used is based on the fact that a defender inside a hill fort slinging his stones downwards can sling further than his attacker who has to sling upwards. By using at least two ramparts and slinging from the inner rampart it was possible for the defenders to hit the attackers although they themselves were out of range. Thus forts with two ramparts (bi-vallate) or three ramparts or more (multi-vallate) were constructed.

Some idea of the scale of action involved is that in two pits alone at Maiden Castle 40,000 sling-stones were found.

It is self-evident that for effective slingstone warfare forts on gradual slopes had to have their ramparts further apart than those on steep ground: i.e., Hod Hill (very steep) the ramparts being 60 yards apart whilst at Badbury Rings, a slighter slope, they are 100 yards apart.

These forts served a very useful purpose from Neolithic times to late Iron Age but with the coming of the Romans under Vespasian in AD 43 with their advanced techniques the forts were one by one subdued and although a few were garrisoned by the Romans for a while, they gradually fell into disuse and were abandoned.

With the departure of the Romans and the coming of the Dark Ages knowledge of what these forts were and who had made them was lost and we have a period of a thousand years during which nobody seems to have known or cared about these beautiful places. Even the early map-makers such as Saxton, Norden and Speed completely ignored them. The first antiquarian to ponder over these forts was Dr William Stukeley who in 1724 published his *Itinerarium Curiosum* and drew the attention of the learned world to them. His *Abury* — Avebury — is the finest early example of detailed archaeological fieldwork.

These inspired Sir Richard Colt Hoare of Stourhead who in the early years of the 19th century gave up fox-hunting in favour of hunting earth-works. His findings he recorded in his volumes on *Ancient Wiltshire* together with some beautifully engraved plans of several of the earthworks of the Cranborne Chase.

The method of construction was to mark out the plan by means of a setting-out ditch, examples of which may still be seen. After this the main ditch was built, the top soil being dumped into the interior and the chalk dug out used for the actual rampart. Now one has only to look at forts such as Old Sarum, Figsbury Rings and others to see the enormous amount of earth which had to be moved by people possessed only of antler picks and reed baskets. It is obvious that the population must have been much larger than is popularly supposed. Thousands of workers over a considerable period of time must have been required to build the larger forts; even so it is clear that different sections were frequently built by different gangs and then joined badly. The ramparts themselves were composed in the main of the local underlying material — limestone, sandstone or, as in the greater part of Wiltshire, chalk. Even in the chalk areas sarsen stones were frequently found and these often used to strengthen the ramparts. Oolite was used at Maiden Castle and nearby Chalbury. It would appear that sometimes the ramparts were revetted on the outside with timbers as at Maiden Castle and Bindon Hill beach-head.

Obviously the weakest points of defence were the entrances and much thought was given to their construction. Frequently the entrance banks are turned inwards to expose the invaders. This is clearly seen at the west and north-east entrances to Hod Hill, the south-west entrance to Hambledon and many others.

The actual entrances usually had a timber-built gateway of great strength. In some, such as Maiden Castle, the entrances were flanked by walls built of oolitic limestone. One of the most remarkable facts about these forts, to the author's mind, is that, although many are nearly four thousand years old, the vast majority are still well preserved. It may be that they were in remote places, high up, and were difficult to plough, but despite this our ancestors during all this period deserve great praise for the care they took to preserve them for posterity.

It is ironic that in our own time when we really understand and appreciate the great monuments to the distant past that the greatest danger to their survival has arisen. Modern equipment has enabled farmers to plough where no man could before and this together with the subsidy for ploughing and the shortage of land has produced a very real threat to their safety. One such example is that on Hambledon Hill, a neolithic causewayed camp was ploughed out about 1960 and lost forever. Let us hope that more enlightened views may prevail and that this heritage from our past may be preserved for all time.

Ackling Dyke Woodyates to Salisbury. Sheet 184, grid reference 199033, then north-eastwards. ACCESS RIGHTS: Public rights of way along most of its length. *Park beside the A354, Salisbury to Blandford road, in the layby on the north side just before the hamlet of Woodyates on the Dorset border. Ackling Dyke can be clearly seen, going into the dip and following the side of the wood, and its course is fully described in the section that follows.* ARCHAEOLOGY: The Ackling Dyke between Old Sarum and Badbury is one of the finest preserved sections of Roman road in the country. It consists of a raised road with side ditches 84 feet apart. At the commencement of the Wiltshire section the raised road can easily be seen from the large lay-by. Take the track leading from the rear of the lay-by and go through an iron gateway on your right which leads directly onto the Roman road. Follow the Roman road for some 700 yards after commencing the walk when you will meet a wood on your left. Turn right into the wood following the line of the road. Now follow an easy and obvious path through the wood until you finally emerge onto a minor road. Cross this and take the right hand path of two paths facing you passing a rubbish tip. Once more the path is clear and easy to follow passing through Knighton Wood. After passing Knighton Wood Farm on your right you come to a metalled road. The Roman road continues across the fields facing you but at this point it is easier to turn left up the road for about 300 yards before turning right along an ox drove. Continue along this track in a direction only slightly north of east. Go past an obvious track leading off to

Ackling Dyke : causeway across the downs

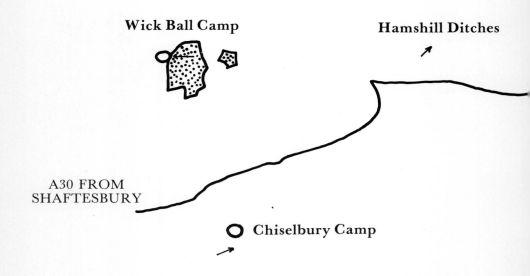

Wick Ball Camp

Hamshill Ditches

A30 FROM SHAFTESBURY

Chiselbury Camp

Listed sites around
ACKLING DYKE ROMAN ROAD

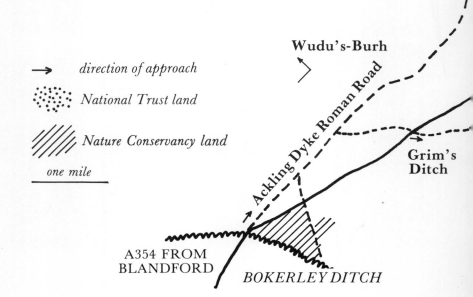

→ *direction of approach*

⋯ *National Trust land*

/// *Nature Conservancy land*

—— *one mile*

Wudu's-Burh

Ackling Dyke Roman Road

Grim's Ditch

A354 FROM BLANDFORD

BOKERLEY DITCH

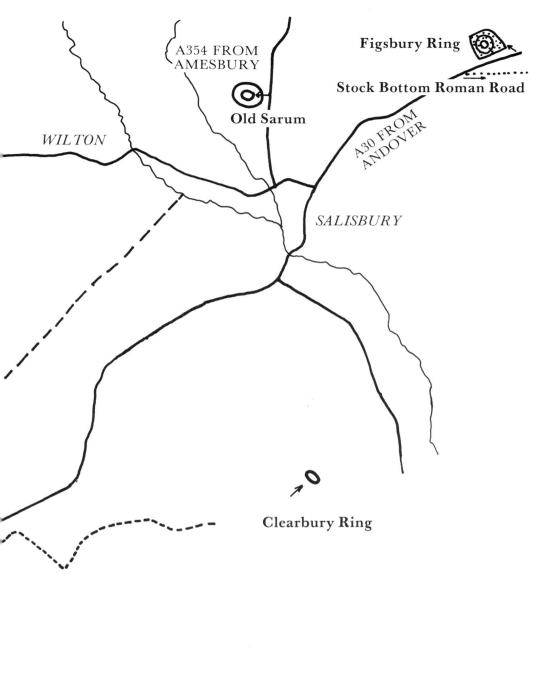

A354 FROM AMESBURY

Figsbury Ring

Stock Bottom Roman Road

Old Sarum

WILTON

A30 FROM ANDOVER

SALISBURY

Clearbury Ring

your left and a quarter of a mile further on one to your right. A half mile further on you will reach a cross roads with building on your right hand. Take the left hand track through a five-barred iron gate. This track leads northwards and directly down to Bishopstone where excellent refreshments may be obtained at the White Hart. At Bishopstone take the road to the right to Stratford Tony. Do not take the first turning on the left opposite Throop Manor House but continue on to just outside Stratford Tony. Here is a road to the left leading to Wilton. This road follows directly the line of the old Roman road although it is no longer visible. After a short distance a T-junction is reached. Go straight across following an obvious path up a straight hill negotiating a metal barrier. The path is now once more fairly clear. Be sure to pass to the right of two small copses. About a mile after leaving you will come across a small gypsy encampment. Turn left here and carry on for two hundred yards on the main road. The race course is now quite clear. Cross this and walk onto the golf course. Head for the left hand side of a line of trees in a north-westerly direction which will bring you out onto a path leading to the club house. Pass this and go along the track to the main road A3094. Cross the A3094 and follow the signpost to Bemerton; turn right towards Salisbury and take the A345 out to Old Sarum. Note: A compass should be taken as it is very easy to lose one's way if bad weather should crop up. The Ordnance map is also essential and the walk should not be taken in wet weather as the mud is very thick. SOIL AND CULTIVA-TION: Chalk; lengths of open downland or undergrowth but other parts reduced to dirt tracks or ploughed out. NEARBY LISTED SITES: Wudu-Burh, Grim's Ditch, Clearbury Ring. OTHER PLACES OF INTEREST: Bokerley Ditch, mentioned under the Grim's Ditch entry. Stratford Tony, the "street-ford" bridging point of the Roman road, has a beautiful church with an original stone altar and a mass dial. REFRESHMENT: Obtainable at the White Horse in Bishopstone.

Adam and Eve The Long Stones, Beckhampton, near Avebury. Sheet 173, grid reference 089693. Early Bronze Age sacred monument, about 2500 to 2000 BC. ACCESS RIGHTS: None; but these two large sarsens are clearly visible from a public road immediately to the south of their field. *Turn off the A36 midway between Avebury and the Beckhampton roundabout, northward into the hamlet of Avebury Trusloe. You pass a small housing estate and then come to a crossroads. Turn left here, into a narrow lane. You will see the stones in half a mile, in the field opposite the farm buildings.* ARCHAEOLOGY: As with the Avebury stones, one is a lozenge shape and the other a rounded upright. But until the 18th century there were three stones in this grouping, the third being broken up by Richard Fowler whose vandalism was condemned by William Stukeley. They may have comprised a U-shaped setting or cove, but it is equally likely they were part of the stone avenue which Stukeley found extending to Beckhampton. Adam, the larger lozenge-shaped one, fell in 1911. When it was re-erected the crouched skeleton of a middle-aged man, with a Bronze Age beaker which had contained his food for the journey to the next world, was found at its base. SOIL AND CULTIVATION: Chalk, ploughed to edge of stones. NEARBY LISTED SITES: Beckhampton Long Barrow, Avebury, Windmill Hill, Silbury Hill, West Kennett Long Barrow, Kennett Stone Avenue, Beckhampton Roman Road. OTHER PLACES OF INTEREST, AND REFRESHMENTS: See under Avebury.

Adam and Eve : sacred stones, perhaps once part of an avenue from Avebury to Beckhampton

Adam's Grave Pewsey Downs, near Pewsey. Sheet 173, grid reference 113634. Late Neolithic chambered long barrow, about 3000 to 2500 BC. ACCESS RIGHTS: In the Pewsey Downs National Nature Reserve, open freely. *Turn off the A345 at Pewsey, north-west to Wilcot Green and cross the Kennet and Avon Canal. Keep on this road to Alton Priors, where you turn right at the crossroads and drive uphill on to the downs. Park almost at the top, in the layby on your left, and walk about 40 yards back down the hill to a National Nature Reserve notice and stile. Adam's Grave is on the summit of the hill, overlooking this point.* ARCHAEOLOGY: Wedge-shaped grave 200 feet long by 100 feet wide and 20 feet high, displaying the highly successful utilisation of a natural landmark to give the barrow an appearance of great length. It blends Cotswold and Wessex methods of construction. There is a kerb of oolitic dry walling but the magnificent side ditches are a feature of long barrows on the Wessex chalk. The sarsen burial chamber exposed at the south-east was opened in 1860 and contained several skeletons and a leaf arrowhead. Adam's Grave was formerly Wodnesbeorge, otherwise Woden's Beorh, and is the traditional site of the battle in 592 AD between the Saxons of Wessex and those of Ceawlin of the upper Thames Valley. The Anglo-Saxon Chronicle records that there was "a great slaughter" here. To see the barrow in its superb setting you can keep on the path leftwards to the summit of Milk Hill. On the side of this hill is a splendid White Horse carved out of the chalk by Robert Pile, a local farmer, in 1812. SOIL AND CULTIVATION: Chalk; open downland. NEARBY LISTED SITES: Knap Hill, Wansdyke, Swanborough Tump. OTHER PLACES OF INTEREST: Alton Barnes is a charming village with a church which is redundant but well preserved and open to visitors. Note as you enter that the chancel is out of line with the nave, being to the left. This is alternately put down to variation in the magnetic compass, alignment on sunrise at different times of the year, and the memory of Christ's head falling to the left after death on the cross. There is a simple beauty about this church which is very appealing. Note the Mass dial on the tower near the entrance door. It is much worn but can still be made out, reminding us of days when there were no clocks and watches and times of service had to be measured by sun and shade. The walls are Saxon work with long and short quoins all the way up. Only a mile away is the lovely village of Alton Priors with its splendid church. Note the amusing brass to William Butten with William about to enter the gates of heaven. There is an earlier brass of a lady in girdled gown, from which a quaint ornament is hanging. REFRESHMENTS: As Devizes is the nearest point, the traveller is advised to carry refreshment and take the opportunity for a fuller exploration of the chalkland flowers and other delights of the Pewsey Downs National Nature Reserve, where you can eat on the summit of Milk Hill and contemplate the whole beauty of the setting and its beautiful scenery in all directions.

Aldbourne Four Barrows Sugar Hill, Aldbourne, near Hungerford. Sheet 174, grid reference 249774. Bronze Age barrow cemetery, 2500 to 1500 BC. ACCESS RIGHTS: Beside public right-of-way across the hilltop. *Park in Aldbourne, on the A419 Hungerford to Swindon road. Walk uphill by the parish church, on the track northward on to the downs. This climbs for nearly two miles, along a ridge. The Four Barrows are at the summit, before the wood.* ARCHAEOLOGY: Important barrow group, the contents of which are in the British Museum. Three of the four mounds, all eight to ten feet high, are the Wessex bell-type of round barrow which has the distinguishing feature of a flat area between its mound and ditch. These touch and are in a line. The fourth is an ordinary bowl-shaped mound, also ten feet high. They were excavated by W. Greenwell near the end of the last century. Two of the bell barrows contained cremations and the third a skeleton. Other finds included amber, beads, tanged flint arrowhead, fragment of greenstone axe, and a grooved dagger. The bowl barrow had a cremation in a burial cist covered with four sarsen stones. But the famous Aldbourne barrow is at the foot of this hill, in the field beside the A419 just north of the wood. It is a bowl about 100 feet across by six feet high, and appears smoothed by ploughing though it is now marked around the edge by stakes and preserved under grass amongst the barley. This mound gave the British Museum its Aldbourne cup, an incense cup with lid, and two bronze awls, a bronze dagger, and beads of faience, amber, fossils and shale. To the north of it was another cremation

Aldbourne : the barrow at the foot of Sugar Hill. Its fine cups are in the British Museum

accompanied with a lidless incense cup and two arrowheads, one barbed and tanged and the other triangular, as well as flint flakes. SOIL AND CULTIVATION: Chalk; grass. NEARBY LISTED SITES: Upper Upham Field System, Membury Fort, Littlecote Roman Mosaic, Liddington Long Barrow. OTHER PLACES OF INTEREST: Aldbourne has been awarded the prize by the Countryside Commission for the best kept village in Wiltshire. It is certainly very beautiful with its village green and pond. The church is outstanding, and has splendid pre-reformation memorials to priests. One to Henry Frekylton is a brass of 1508 on the chancel floor but the finest is to John Store whose alabaster tomb cover shows him over six feet, lying on vestments and holding a chalice. Littlecote House, just by Chilton Foliat, is open daily and should not be missed. REFRESHMENTS: Excellent meals at the Crown Hotel, Aldbourne, or the Bear Hotel, Hungerford.

Avebury Stone Circles Avebury, near Marlborough. Sheet 173, grid reference 103700. Neolithic and Early Bronze Age stone circles inside henge monument, about 3000 to 2000 BC. ACCESS RIGHTS: National Trust land, in the guardianship of the Department of the Environment, open freely. Avebury has its own museum, by the churchyard. *Turn north from the A4 at Beckhampton roundabout, seven miles west of Marlborough, on to the A36 towards Swindon. In a mile you come to Avebury's two acre car park, on the left 200 yards outside the earthwork.* ARCHAEOLOGY: A great bank of chalk 1400 feet in diameter and 18 feet high, known to archaeologists as a henge, encloses 28 acres of flat ground. On the inside is a quarry ditch 15 feet deep. It was originally twice as deep. There were four entrances, the eastern and the western ones being serviced by ceremonial avenues of stones, and each now has a road. In the enclosure was a great circle of sarsen boulders, the largest of the Grey Wethers, brought on rollers from the Marlborough Downs, alternating between lozenge-shaped stones and simpler pillars. Some weigh over 40 tons. There were originally 100 stones, of which 30 remain. Many of these in the eastern half were buried in the middle ages when a village was established inside the earthworks. They were dug up by Alexander Keiller between 1934 and 1939. Beneath one was a mediaeval barber, killed

continued on page 17

Avebury : outer circle, and the ditch, in the best preserved south-west section

13

Avebury : from the northern edge of the main circle, drawn by William Stukeley in 1722

Avebury : Stukeley's drawing of the south circle

14

Avebury : view from the north of the Cove, 1721

Avebury : outer and inner circles

View of the Cell of the Celtic Temple at Abury. Aug.t 15. 1721

The Cove of the Northern temple.

Avebury : the Cove has been only two stones since William Stukeley's time, but originally it was a U-shaped setting of three giant sarsens

Avebury : the Cove in the 1920s

16

Avebury : the Cove looking less rustic in the 1980s

Avebury : 18th century print of lozenge-shaped stones in the main circle

when the stone he was removing fell on to him. John Aubrey, the antiquary, discovered Avebury in 1649 and took Charles II to see the monument, after the king heard Aubrey's claim that Avebury "did as much excell Stonehenge as a cathedral does a parish church". In his *Monumenta Britannica,* a vast compilation which was not put into print until three hundred years later, Aubrey describes how the mighty stones were broken up by fires — "after the stone is well heated, draw a line with cold water and

Listed sites around
AVEBURY

Windmill Hill

*A4 FROM
CALNE*

Oldbury Castle

Adam and Eve

Beckhampton Long Barrow

**Beckhampton
Roman
Road**

Wansdyke

*A361 FROM
DEVIZES*

one mile

National Trust land

//// Nature Conservancy land

→ *direction of approach*

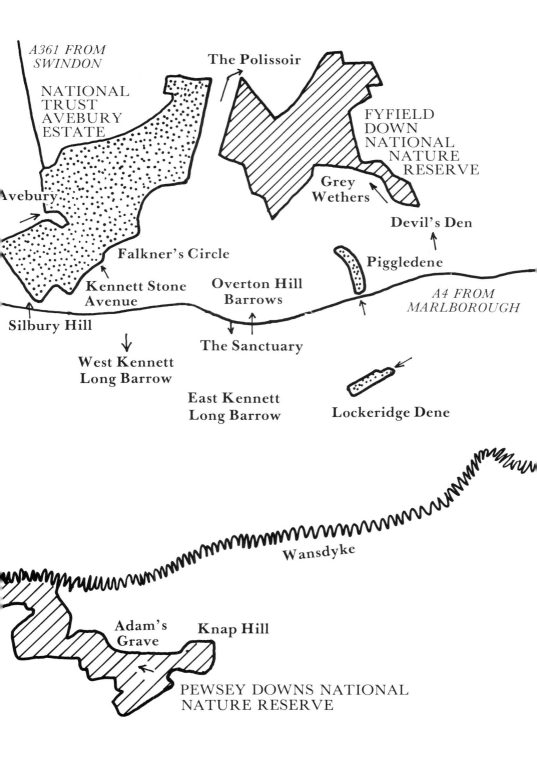

A361 FROM SWINDON

NATIONAL TRUST AVEBURY ESTATE

The Polissoir

FYFIELD DOWN NATIONAL NATURE RESERVE

Avebury

Grey Wethers

Devil's Den

Falkner's Circle

Piggledene

A4 FROM MARLBOROUGH

Kennett Stone Avenue

Overton Hill Barrows

Silbury Hill

The Sanctuary

West Kennett Long Barrow

East Kennett Long Barrow

Lockeridge Dene

Wansdyke

Adam's Grave

Knap Hill

PEWSEY DOWNS NATIONAL NATURE RESERVE

immediately give a knock with a smith's sledge, and it will break like collets (collar-bands) at the glass-house''. They did this to provide building stone and clear their land, and the empty grassland of Avebury's eastern half shows how successful they were. Inside the great circle were two other stone circles, each of about 30 stones and with a diameter of 350 feet. Only nine of these stones survive, two of them fallen. Inside the circles were other settings of stones. The arrangement on the opposite side of the road from the Red Lion car park is now reduced to two large blocks. Until the 18th century there was a third, making a U-shaped arrangement known to archaeologists as a cove, though they can give no explanation of its purpose. The south circle still has an off-centre D-shaped setting, with six surviving stones and another six marked by concrete pillars. By Avebury standards this little grouping was of very small size. On the northern edge of the great circle, where the Swindon road leaves the earthwork, there are three concrete markers of stones which did not form part of the main circle. They may represent an earlier stone circle, demolished in antiquity to allow the building of the henge, but an absence of other holes on the same arc suggests that it was never completed in any case. Any description of Avebury has to dwell on its physical remains. We know so little of its actual use and purpose. It was obviously a great centre of religious culture and ceremonial. Even today it cannot be seen in isolation, and the whole complex must have incorporated the stones, circles and barrows of the surrounding landscape. By Iron Age or Roman times it had lost some of its sanctity and unlike the Stonehenge surroundings its ground was put under the plough, even inside the circles. With the coming of Christian times the local church was not built inside the sacred circle, as was the case at Knowlton Rings in Dorset, but placed just beyond the earthworks — perhaps out of concern for a distant folk memory of Avebury's pagan past. Until recent years it was National Trust policy to advocate the clearance of the cottages inside the ring, as they became vacant, to restore the original appearance of the site. This plan has now been dropped, however, and the buildings are regarded in their own way as being as much part of the history of Avebury as the stones. SOIL AND CULTIVATION: Chalk, grassland. NEARBY LISTED SITES: Kennett Stone Avenue, Falkner's Circle, The Sanctuary, Overton Hill, West Kennett Long Barrow, Silbury

Hill, Beckhampton Long Barrow, Adam and Eve Stones, Windmill Hill, The Polissoir. OTHER PLACES OF INTEREST: Parish church of St James at Avebury, which has a lot of Anglo-Saxon features. It was probably built about the middle of the 10th century and then much altered after the arrival of the Normans. Aisles were added in the 12th century. The crowning glory is the rood loft and it is one of the very few to have survived the Reformation. The Catholic parishioners, hearing of what was happening elsewhere, hid the screen behind a lathe and plaster covering against the east wall of the nave above the chancel arch. It was rediscovered in 1810 and has been repainted in its original colours. The screen below is Victorian. Avebury Manor, approached from the Swindon exit from the monument, is open daily to the public from June to August. It was built on the site of monastic buildings in 1601, and has panelled rooms, impressive original chimneys, and moulded ceilings. The next village north from Avebury, Winterbourne Monkton, has lost most of its ancient monuments but the church is worth a look, if only to see the fine Norman font. REFRESHMENTS: The Red Lion is conveniently at the heart of Avebury, and there are excellent inns at Marlborough if you are using the town as a base for these explorations.

Barbury Castle Wroughton, near Swindon. Sheet 173, grid reference 149763. Iron Age hill-fort, about 150 BC. ACCESS DETAILS: In Wiltshire County Council's Barbury Country Park, freely open. *Turn off the A361 Avebury to Swindon road at Wroughton, on to the B4005. Continue straight ahead in a mile at Burderop, along the road beside the turnpike toll-house. Barbury is on the top of the escarpment.* ARCHAEOLOGY: The track across the top through Barbury is the prehistoric ridgeway, the oldest road in Britain. Double

Barbury Castle : impressive earthworks now a country park

ramparts and ditches with outworks at the east entrance make this a strongly defended point. Nearly 12 acres are enclosed, and appear to have been occupied as a town. Huts and storage pits show up on aerial photographs. Finds from the fort are in the Mount House Museum at Marlborough College. As with many hill-forts it is a delightful place for a picnic with wide views, into the Midlands. There is a memorial to Richard Jefferies, the great nature writer who was born at Coate, which as you look down is at the near-right of the sprawl of Swindon, on the outskirts behind the reservoir. The wood at the foot of Barbury, a third of a mile northwards towards Wroughton Airfield, is of particular interest. In the field to the left of it, between the wood and the road from the airfield, the battle of Beranburh was fought in 556. The Anglo Saxon Chronicle records: "In this year Cynric and Caewlin fought against the Britons at Beranburh". SOIL AND CULTIVATION: Chalk; open downland. NEARBY LISTED SITES: Lid-

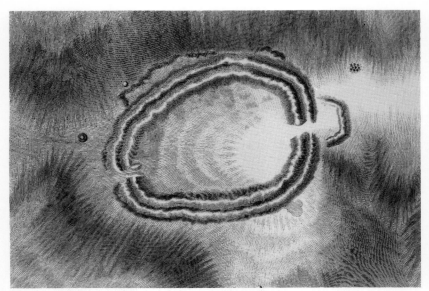

Barbury Castle : plan from Colt Hoare's *Ancient Wiltshire* 1819 volume

dington Castle, Coate Stone Circle, The Polissoir. OTHER PLACES OF
INTEREST: White Horse, above Broad Hinton off A361 between
Wroughton and Avebury, one of the six cut in Wiltshire in Victorian times.
It is 78 feet long, cut by William Simmonds of Littleton Farm in 1864 —
and was covered by hedgecuttings and soil during the war years to prevent
its use as a landmark by enemy bombers. A visit to Wroughton church,
which has its pre-Reformation sanctus bell still in position, is also recommended. REFRESHMENTS: Wroughton or Avebury.

Battlesbury Hill Bishopstrow, near Warminster. Sheet 184, grid reference
897457. Iron Age hill-fort, about 80 BC to 43 AD. ACCESS RIGHTS:
Public footpath follows much of the outer rampart, along the southern and
western sides. *Follow the A36 eastward from Warminster for about a mile. On the
Warminster side of Bishopstrow House, on the north side of the road at the centre of a
length of high stone wall, there is a farm road to Home Farm. This is a public path.
Half a mile after it crosses the railway you turn left, on to another path up the centre of
the ridge. This leads to the entrance into the fort, through outworks at the north-east
corner.* ARCHAEOLOGY: Triple banked, stoutly enclosing 24 acres.
Probably held a permanent settlement, rather than being a refuge only in
times of tension. Excavations of pits have revealed considerable quantities
of late Iron Age domestic and warfare debris, ranging from querns and a
door-latch to hoops from chariot wheels and clay sling-bullets. The public
path turns to follow the southern edge of the fort, overlooking Warminster,
before heading across the top of the downs to the upper part of the School of
Infantry. Just outside the north-west entrance, in a pit, was the mass grave
of men, women and a child. It is thought that they were slaughtered by the
Roman swordsmen of Vespasian's Second Legion at the time of the con-
quest. SOIL AND CULTIVATION: Chalk; banks unspoilt downland but

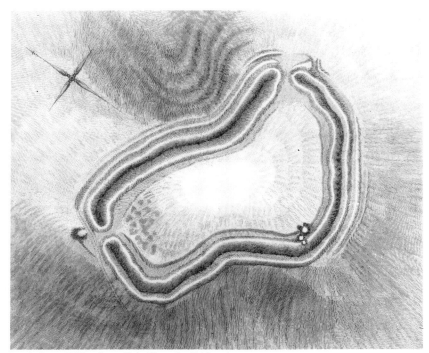

Battlesbury Hill : from Colt Hoare's 1812 volume

Battlesbury : whole hill encircled by massive triple banks

the interior is arable. NEARBY LISTED SITES: Scratchbury Hill, Middle Hill, Cley Hill, Westbury White Horse, Bratton Castle. OTHER PLACES OF INTEREST, AND REFRESHMENTS: See under Scratchbury Hill.

Beckhampton Long Barrow Avebury, near Marlborough. Sheet 173, grid reference 087692. Neolithic long barrow, about 4000 to 3500 BC. ACCESS RIGHTS: Visible from roundabout and a right-of-way behind the barrow. *Turn off the A36 midway between Avebury and the Beckhampton roundabout, northward into the hamlet of Avebury Trusloe. You pass a small housing estate and then come to a crossroads. Turn left here, into a narrow lane. You pass the Adam and Eve stones and farm buildings in half a mile, and park here. Continue along the grass lane for a short distance leftward at the corner. The barrow is visible after the gate, on the other side of the hedge.* ARCHAEOLOGY: Important in its own right, as a

23

Beckhampton Long Barrow : large but mutilated

mound 225 feet long by 120 feet wide and 15 feet high, and also as the terminus of the second stone avenue out of Avebury that was still traceable in William Stukeley's time. The barrow must be broadly contemporary with the Windmill Hill peoples and it is possible there was a timber or stone structure similar to the Sanctuary in this vicinity. Although the mound is large enough to hide burial chambers this seems unlikely, as despite the obviously heavy disturbance there are no signs of sarsens protruding from the ground. It must be assumed to be an earthen barrow, which had timber rather than stone mortuary chambers. Excavation has failed to reveal the primary burials, though it did uncover one of the Beaker folk who was buried in the side when the mound was already old. SOIL AND CULTIVATION: Chalk; overgrown in grassland. NEARBY LISTED SITES: Adam and Eve Stones, Avebury, Windmill Hill, Silbury Hill, West Kennett Long Barrow, Kennett Stone Avenue, Beckhampton Roman Road. OTHER PLACES OF INTEREST, AND REFRESHMENTS: See under Avebury.

Beckhampton Roman Road Avebury, near Marlborough. Sheet 173, grid reference 077684. Preserved Roman roadway, from 55 AD. ACCESS RIGHTS: Visible beside main road, but although it is a length of Roman road there is strangely no present day right-of-way along it. *On level ground on the east side of the A361 nearly a mile on the Devizes side of the Beckhampton roundabout. Points towards Silbury Hill. Layby nearly opposite, on west side of the road.* ARCHAEOLOGY: This length of raised carriageway carried the Roman road from London to Bath and is the best preserved section on the Marlborough Downs. About 300 yards survive, about 25 feet across and three feet high. Subject to an Environment Department preservation order. SOIL AND CULTIVATION: Chalk; grassed, ploughed to edge. NEARBY LISTED SITES: Beckhampton Long Barrow, Adam and Eve Stones, Avebury Stone Circles, Silbury Hill, West Kennett Long Barrow, Wansdyke, Oldbury Castle. OTHER PLACES OF INTEREST, AND REFRESHMENTS: See under Avebury.

Bratton Castle Bratton, near Westbury. Sheet 184, grid reference 900516. Iron Age hill-fort about 20 BC, and Neolithic long barrow about 4000 to 3500 BC. ACCESS RIGHTS: In guardianship of the Environment Department, always open. *Turn off the B3098 three miles east of Westbury, at the west end of Bratton village. Drive uphill and through the centre of the castle to the parking area on the far side. The long barrow is close to this point, on the other side of the banks.* ARCHAEOLOGY: Large double-banked earthworks enclosing 25 acres. Few finds except quernstones for corn grinding and a cartload of slingstone

Beckhampton Roman Road : heads straight for Silbury Hill

Bratton Castle : double banked hill-fort

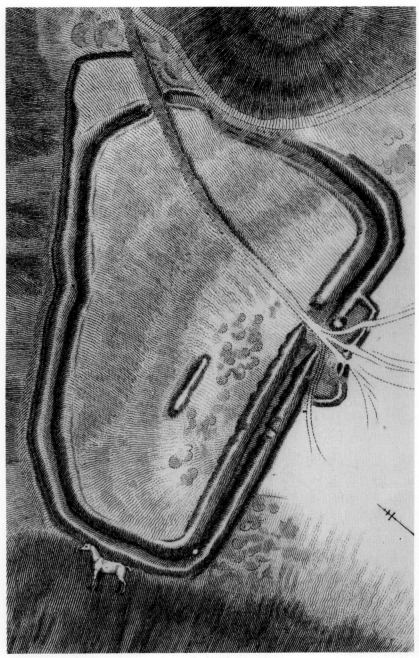

Bratton Castle : plan from Sir Richard Colt Hoare's *Ancient Wiltshire,* 1812 volume

Bratton Castle : long barrow, pitted by digging

pebbles. The long barrow is pitted from excavations, which revealed two skeletons which had been partly burnt, in a timber mortuary chamber at the east end. It is still impressive, about 230 feet long, 65 feet wide and 12 feet high. SOIL AND CULTIVATION: Chalk; the interior of the fort has been ploughed and seeded back to grass. NEARBY LISTED SITES: Westbury White Horse, Cley Hill, Battlesbury Hill, Middle Hill, Scratchbury Hill. OTHER PLACES OF INTEREST, AND REFRESHMENTS, See under Westbury White Horse.

Casterley Camp Upavon, near Pewsey. Sheet 184, grid reference 116534. Iron Age fortified enclosure, about 50 BC and throughout Roman times to 450 AD. ACCESS RIGHTS: Public path beside the southern rampart, but this track is closed when the red flags are flying as the site is on the edge of the army's Larkhill impact area. *The junction of the A342 with the A45 is at Upavon. Turn on to the A342, Devizes road, for a third of a mile. Then west, uphill, along the minor road signed "Widdington 1" and "Casterley A/4 Range and Demolition". Continue straight ahead at the turn to Widdington Farm and drive for a mile to the red army gate and range office. Park on the verge just before the gate. Read the*

Casterley Camp : encloses massive area

27

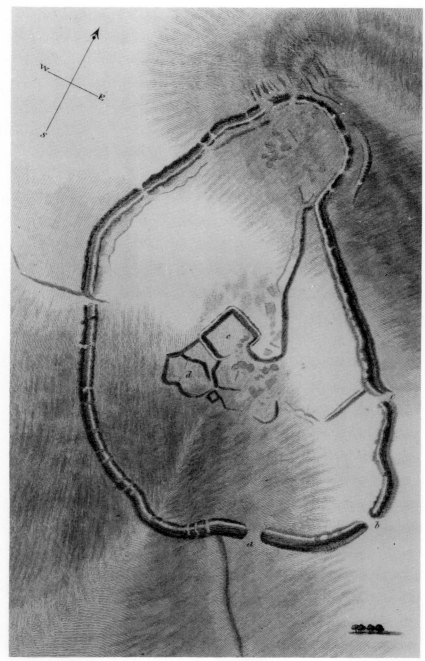

Casterley Camp : plan from Colt Hoare's *Ancient Wiltshire*, 1812

notices: "Keep out when red flags are flying". Other times — usually evenings, weekends and block-leave periods — the Imber Ranges perimeter path is open for use. If this is the case go through the gate and turn left on to the wide dirt track. For half a mile it skirts the bank of the camp. ARCHAEOLOGY: "Catterley Banks" as the locals call it has a comparatively low rampart, five feet high, but is massive in extent, enclosing 62 acres. The sunken trackways into it are contemporary with the bank and connect the settlement with Celtic field systems. The rampart curves outwards at the north-east to cover a blind-spot, the approach up a dry valley, and shows that the earthwork was of a defensive nature. Air photographs have revealed ditches, pits and other signs of occupation across the interior. Brooches and other material from 1909-12 excavations, including Roman Samian pottery, are in Devizes Museum. SOIL AND CULTIVATION: Chalk; banks and outworks downland, interior ploughed and under cereals. NEARBY LISTED SITES: Sidbury Hill, Gallows Barrow. OTHER PLACES OF INTEREST: Enford, on the A345, has a church of great architectural beauty, scratch dial on the porch, and an exquisite monument to Jennifer Baskerville. There is a broken preaching cross. REFRESHMENTS: Ample at Pewsey, five miles north.

Castle Ditches Ansty, near Tisbury. Sheet 184, grid reference 963283. Iron Age hill-fort, from about 75 BC. ACCESS RIGHTS: Encircled by public paths, but ask at the farm for permission to walk on the hilltop. *Turn off the A30 midway between Shaftesbury and Wilton, northwards through Ansty until you reach a T-junction. Turn left and follow the road for about a quarter mile to another junction. Turn right here and pass Unicorn Cottage. Turn right opposite a cottage and bungalow, to Withyslade Farm. A tarred public road leads to the farm, where you park. Public trackways fork left and right around the base of the hill. An alternative route is a third of a mile further north along the other road, where a dirt track crosses a stream and goes to the left of a thatched cottage into Haredene Wood. It is an attractive walk of a mile through the trees to the hill.* ARCHAEOLOGY: A flat-topped hill with massive fortifications, strong double banks that enclose 24 acres. There are triple ramparts on the less steep south-east slope. SOIL AND CULTIVATION: Chalk; banks mainly wooded, interior ploughed. NEARBY LISTED SITES: Wick Ball Camp, Chiselbury Camp, Wudu-Burh, White Sheet Hill at Ansty, Winklebury Hill. OTHER PLACES OF INTEREST: Old Wardour Castle, at the back of Ansty village, is a magnifi-

Castle Ditches : strongly defended plateau

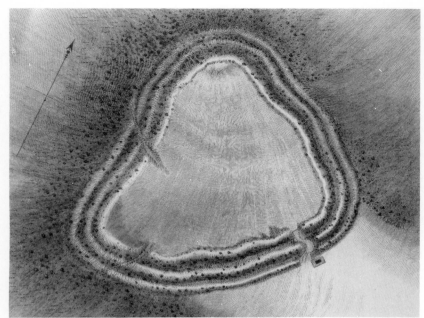

Castle Ditches : plan from Colt Hoare's *Ancient Wiltshire*, 1812 volume

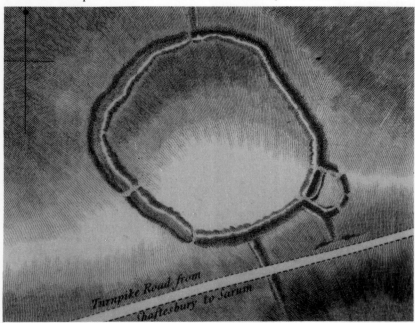

Chiselbury Camp : from *Ancient Wiltshire*, 1812, showing that the turnpiked main road then passed the earthworks

cent ruin of Lord Lovel's 1393 fortified house in its post Civil War siege condition. It was given all the flavour of a picturesque ruin with 18th century parkland and grotto. Opened by the Environment Department; ask for key to see the historic privy. Ansty church has 17th century bench-ends. Tisbury has a splendid church with several fine brasses. REFRESHMENTS: Excellent public houses in many of the villages, including Ansty and Ludwell, and at Tisbury.

Chiselbury Camp Fovant, near Wilton. Sheet 184, grid reference 018282. Iron Age hill-fort, from about 200 BC. ACCESS RIGHTS: East ditch skirted by a public path. *Turn south from the A30 a quarter mile west of Fovant, along the lane signed to "Fifield, Bowerchalke". At the top of the hill there is a straight track to the left, beside a line of cypress trees. In a mile and a half, just after you have passed the fort, there is a gate and stile and a path leading to the earthworks.* ARCHAEOLOGY: Circular single banked hill-fort, with double ramparts on the vulnerable south-west side, enclosing nine acres. Recently potsherds have been found of both the building period and later Belgic occupation. Outstanding viewpoint, at 650 feet, overlooking the Nadder valley from a steep escarpment. SOIL AND CULTIVATION: Chalk; banks downland but interior ploughed and seeded back to grass. NEARBY LISTED SITES: Wick Ball Camp, Hamshill Ditches, Castle Ditches, Wudu-Burh. OTHER PLACES OF INTEREST: Compton Chamberlayne, two miles east of Fovant, is a beautiful village with its church set in the grounds of Compton House. Fovant itself is pretty, with its stream dammed into a large pond. REFRESHMENTS: In the centre of Fovant are two very good hotels which serve meals.

Chiselbury Camp : enclosed by circular ditch and bank

Clearbury Ring Charlton, near Downton. Sheet 184, grid reference 153244. Iron Age hill-fort, about 250 BC. ACCESS RIGHTS: Public path around most of the outer edge. *Turn off the A338, Fordingbridge road, two miles south of Salisbury, to Odstock. In Odstock village turn towards the Yew Tree and*

"Whitsbury Down 2" at the crossroads. *On the top of the down, after the wood, you reach a house and the road turns into a dirt track. Continue along it for about a third of a mile to the arable field on the left of the corner. A public bridleway leads along the grassy edge of the field, following the hedgerow to Clearbury — which is the clump on the skyline. The right of way follows the earthworks, to the right.* ARCHAEOLOGY: Small but interesting fort of five acres which is a beautiful landmark. SOIL AND CULTIVATION: Chalk; banks mainly open downland, but the interior covered with beech trees. NEARBY LISTED SITES: Grim's Ditch, Ackling Dyke. OTHER PLACES OF INTEREST: Odstock is an attractive village with an interesting church, its magnificent pulpit dating from 1580. There is a handsome manor house with fine sycamores at its gate. Nunton is another small village with a prettily sited church. REFRESHMENTS: The Yew Tree at Odstock is a world famous restaurant; or at Nunton, where the Radnor Arms provides excellent bar meals.

Cley Hill Sturford, near Warminster. Sheet 183, grid reference 838450. Iron Age hill-fort, about 300 BC. ACCESS RIGHTS: Owned by the National Trust, freely open. *Two miles west of Warminster, above the A362 Frome road. A signpost opposite a wood points to "Cley Hill". You can drive about half a mile to the foot of the hill. The direct path to the summit has been closed due to excessive wear and the alternative route crosses a stile and follows the fencing until this finishes. From here the path leads directly to the summit.* ARCHAEOLOGY: Single-banked with two earlier Bronze Age round barrows on the 17-acre spine of the hill. One of these is silhouetted for miles. The slopes are steeply scarped, with the prehistoric bank half-way up. Quarried on the southern side. SOIL AND CULTIVATION: Chalk; downland. NEARBY LISTED SITES: White Sheet

Cley Hill : prominent earthworks and barrow, the print being from Colt Hoare's *Ancient Wiltshire,* 1812 volume

Hill at Mere, Battlebury Hill, Middle Hill, Scratchbury Hill, Westbury White Horse, Bratton Castle. OTHER PLACES OF INTEREST: Longleat, Elizabethan house with safari park and the present Viscount Weymouth's erotic murals. REFRESHMENTS: Good food is provided at the Royal Oak in Corsley.

Coate Stone Circle Day House Farm, near Swindon. Sheet 173, grid reference 182824. Early Bronze Age stone circle, about 2500 to 2000 BC. ACCESS RIGHTS: Visible beside road. *Coate, which has the Coate Water Country Park, is on the A345 between the roundabout on the south-western outskirts of Swindon and the roundabout with the A419. Turn south from Coate, along the lane off the dual carriageway opposite the Swindon Autopoint and the Post Houe, 200 yards east from the Coate Water roundabout. In a third of a mile you come to Day House Farm. The stones are immediately opposite the barn, beside the road in the field on the left.* ARCHAEOLOGY: Nine fallen sarsens survive, making up an arc of about a third of the original circle. It would have had a diameter of about 130 feet and extended to about the area of the sycamore tree beside the track to the barn. The circle has the distinction of being discovered by the countryside author Richard Jefferies, who was born at Coate Farm in 1848. SOIL AND CULTIVATION: Chalk; grassland. NEARBY LISTED SITES: Liddington Castle, Liddington Long Barrow, Barbury Castle. OTHER PLACES OF INTEREST: The lake at Coate Water Country Park, off the nearby roundabout. REFRESHMENTS: You can do the obvious and join Swindon's oppressive traffic, or try your luck by following the lane under the main roads and into the countryside.

Codford Circle Codford St Mary, near Warminster. Sheet 184, grid reference 983407. ACCESS RIGHTS: Off the public path, so permission to walk up to the ring has to be obtained from the farm. *Turn north from the A36 at Codford St Mary, along the road signed "Chitterne" for quarter of a mile. Here there is a wide entrance, beside the Codford village sign, which leads to East Codford Farm. Park on the left-hand side of the wide entrance. Immediately beside the private farm road there is a green "Public bridleway" sign pointing uphill along a sunken double-hedged trackway. Walk the full length of the path, about a mile. At the end there is an iron gate. Continue to the end of this field. The fence line to the right leads to the bank.*

Codford Circle : on a hilltop overlooking the Wylye valley

ARCHAEOLOGY: Circular single bank, the perfect symmetry of which led Colt Hoare to suspect that it may have been constructed for juridicial or religious ceremonies. Cultivation has filled in the ditch and lowered the bank. It encloses eight acres of a flat hilltop, with views over the Wylye valley. SOIL AND CULTIVATION: Chalk; bank grassed, interior ploughed. NEARBY LISTED SITES: Upton Great Barrow, Yarnbury Castle. OTHER

PLACES OF INTEREST: The Codford villages both have interesting churches. St Peter's has a remarkable piece of Saxon sculpture, part of a stone cross. St Mary's has a pulpit worked into an altar. It used to be in St Mary's, Oxford, and is probably the one from which Cranmer made his recantation. REFRESHMENTS: Bar snacks may be obtained at the George Inn, Codford St Peter, and the Red Lion, Heytesbury.

Cold Kitchen Hill Kingston Deverill, near Mere. Sheet 183, grid reference 847384. Neolithic long barrow, about 4000 to 3000 BC, and an extensive Romano-Celtic temple and cremation area, about 100 to 200 AD. ACCESS RIGHTS: Public right of way passes the long barrow, though the Roman temple is off the public path network. *Kingston Deverill is on the B3095, Longbridge Deverill to Mere road. At Kingston Deverill you turn off towards Maiden Bradley, as far as Whitepits in about half a mile. Here, to the left of the buildings on the north side of the road, there is a track that climbs to the top of the downs. On the summit there is another track, partly ploughed, for about half a mile to the long barrow, a little way beyond the Ordnance Survey pillar. The barrow has concrete markers. The Roman temple is at the top of the hill on the opposite side of the deep-cut valley, with a wood over the hill on its northern edge.* ARCHAEOLOGY: The fine long barrow is 230 feet long by eight feet high with prominent side ditches; known as "Lang beorh" in a Saxon charter. The temple on the opposite hilltop was shown by Cunnington's excavations to have had as many Celtic as Roman connections. Dozens of Romano-Celtic brooches have been found there, including disc-brooches based upon Hadrianic coins and showing shield-carrying soldiers facing spear-throwing horsemen. Others are of the typical Celtic horse-and-rider type. Many were partially burnt, indicating that they fell from corpse-clothes in a funeral pyre. Cold Kitchen as a name implies meatless bones, and nearby Brimsdown an association with fire. A Roman road crosses these hills and a market fair was held on Cold Kitchen Hill in ancient times. Leslie Grinsell has suggested its origins derived from the proximity of the Roman temple. SOIL AND CULTIVATION: Chalk; barrow grass ploughed to edge, temple under barley. NEARBY LISTED SITES: White Sheet Hill at Mere, Cley Hill. OTHER PLACES OF INTEREST: Maiden Bradley, three miles west, is a charming old village with some very fine houses. Bradley House is still the residence of the Duke of Somerset. Near the old priory is the farmhouse of New Mead, birthplace of the Parliamentary general and regicide Edmund Ludlow. REFRESHMENTS: There are good meals available at the inn in Maiden Bradley, or back on the main road at the coffee shop or the inn beside the A303 at the east end of Zeals.

Cricklade Town Walls Cricklade, near Swindon. Sheet 173, grid reference 103932. Saxon fortifications, late 9th century AD. ACCESS RIGHTS: Rights-of-way follow the line of the wall along the eastern edge of the present town, from the River Thames south to Dance Common. *Cricklade is off the A419 midway between Swindon and Cirencester. This road used to divert from the Roman line of Ermin Street to pass through the town centre, but a by-pass has now been built across the meadows which almost precisely restores the Roman line of the road. Turn off the present A419 on to the half mile of its old course into the east of the town. Park opposite the Cricklade Motor Company. Opposite Spital Lane is a path across the meadows signed "Eisey 1". The low Saxon bank is in the field next to the back of the town buildings.* ARCHAEOLOGY: These defences were

Cricklade Town Walls : construction ordered by Alfred the Great

thought to be Roman, particularly as they comprised a stone wall that was a mile and a half long. Professor F.M. Stenton, the great expert on Saxon England, had other ideas. He considered they were Saxon, and of particular importance in that Cricklade has since shrunk in size, leaving the walls clear of the town's building line and free of mediaeval improvements. He has been proved correct. The Town Walls are based upon the River Thames, rather than Ermin Street — on the other side of the river — which would have been the key to the layout of a Roman wall. Excavation in 1949 and 1952 showed that although plenty of Roman tiles and other material was reused in the walls the crucial pottery of the later Saxon period was also present. This confirmed them to be 9th century, and the defences almost certainly date from Alfred the Great's orders for the defence of the West Saxon kingdom. Finds in Cricklade Museum. SOIL AND CULTIVATION: Alluvial; grassland. NEARBY LISTED SITE: Ringsbury Camp. OTHER PLACES OF INTEREST: Lydiard Park, off B4041, which was sold empty to Swindon Corporation but now has a collection of Georgian furniture. Open all year. REFRESHMENTS: In Cricklade, or inns in the villages.

Cunetione or Cunetio Black Field, Mildenhall, near Marlborough. Sheet 174, grid reference 217696. Roman town and fort, about 50 AD onwards. ACCESS RIGHTS: Crossed by public footpath. *Park in Mildenhall village, north of the A4 at the eastern edge of Marlborough. The road to it is from the A345 in the centre of town, uphill opposite the church. Walk eastwards, taking the road across the river. It is unsigned, a hundred yards on the right after the telephone box. Black Field is on the other side, taking its name from the colour given to the soil by the Roman debris. A hundred yards after the bridge, just around the first corner after the bungalow, a public path enters the field beside the telephone exchange and runs parallel to the river — directly away from the centre of Mildenhall — towards the hamlet of Stitchcombe. It follows the hedge and is signposted to Axford. In a third of a mile it gradually edges closer to the river bank.* ARCHAEOLOGY: The area is littered with Roman settlement remains, including Samian and native pottery, tessellated pavement cubes, tiles, bricks, brooches and even fragments of sculpture. Its importance was such that five Roman roads converged on the town. Streets show as cropmarks. A fort has been discovered from air pictures and had a wall with bastions. Cunetio is the name it is given on the map and by archaeologists, but this is the Celtic river name for the Kennet. The town was distinguished by a derivative form — Cunetione or Cunetzione. There is

35

another river Kennet, in East Anglia, and this too was known in Roman times as the Cunetio. SOIL AND CULTIVATION: Chalk; higher slope ploughed and growing cereals, lower part meadow. NEARBY LISTED SITES: Martinsell Hill, Littlecote Roman Mosaic. OTHER PLACES OF INTEREST: Nature trail and picnic area on the Marlborough side of Savernake Forest, off A346. REFRESHMENTS: Ample facilities in Marlborough.

Cursus Larkhill, near Amesbury. Sheet 184, grid reference 120430. Late Neolithic ceremonial way, about 3000 to 2500 BC, and Bronze Age barrows, about 2100 to 1600 BC. ACCESS RIGHTS: National Trust land, freely open. *Approached from the gravel track a quarter mile west of the Stonehenge car park, off the A344. Drive along it towards Larkhill, for about half a mile.* The banks of the Cursus run westwards into the Fargo Plantation. ARCHAEOLOGY: The Cursus is a mile and a half in length, a ceremonial walk between parallel banks, 400 feet apart, contemporary with the earliest phase of Stonehenge. It points towards Woodhenge. Bought by the National Trust after a national appeal in 1928, with additions given by adjoining owners in the 1950s and 60s. Its purpose is unknown, though it got its name because Stukeley thought it was a racecourse for chariots. It is now regarded as an integral part of the Stonehenge religious complex. Similar earthworks exist elsewhere in southern England, the largest being the Dorset Cursus which is over six miles in length. This too has an alignment which bears a distinct relationship with surrounding monuments. The barrows, also on the Trust's land, include large Bronze Age mounds, up to 11 feet high. They contained cremations, urns and axes, which are now in Devizes Museum. SOIL AND CULTIVATION: Chalk; grassland. NEARBY LISTED SITES, PLACES OF INTEREST, REFRESHMENTS: See under Stonehenge.

Cursus : line of barrows beside Stonehenge

Devil's Den Clatford Bottom, Fyfield, near Marlborough. Sheet 173, grid reference 152697. Late Neolithic burial chamber, about 3500 to 2500 BC. ACCESS RIGHTS: Private land, but can be clearly seen from public bridleway. *Park in Fyfield village, on A4 two miles west of Marlborough. Leave your car off the main road, by barn on side road to church. Walk half a mile along the footway beside the A4, towards Marlborough. On the north side of the road opposite Clatford Farm is a farm track signposted as a bridleway to "Devil's Den 1½". It is in fact less than a mile, on the left side of the track after the barn.* ARCHAEOLOGY: Megalithic burial chamber with four large base stones, the big upright being supported by a buttress of concrete (dated 1921) on a low mound. The great capstone is a lump of sarsen three feet thick and ten feet square.

Devil's Den : William Stukeley's 1723 impressions

Devil's Den : the cromlech survives

It is on a tilt, between four and six feet from the ground. This has the appearance of a Welsh-style cromlech, or dolmen, but it was originally covered by a long barrow 230 feet long by 130 feet wide, unusual in being set on a valley floor instead of the skyline. SOIL AND CULTIVATION: Chalk; ploughed to edge in cereal field. NEARBY LISTED SITES: Grey Wethers, The Polissoir, Piggledene, Lockeridge Dene. OTHER PLACES OF INTEREST, AND REFRESHMENTS: See under Silbury Hill.

Durrington Walls Durrington, near Amesbury. Sheet 184, grid reference 150437. Neolithic henge monument, about 2550 BC. ACCESS RIGHTS: Visible either side of A345, part on public grassland between the old and new courses of the main road about 150 yards from Woodhenge. *Turn off the A345 at the last street light just beyond the "Amesbury" sign on the north edge of the town. "Woodhenge" is signposted. Continue straight ahead at the corner beside Woodhenge, on to a stub-end of the old course of the A345, now marked as a no through road. Durrington Walls encloses most of this valley, from the back gardens of the homes on the left to the large road sign and field below the public house on the right.* ARCHAEOLOGY: Originally it consisted of a huge roughly oval bank of chalk about 100 feet wide at the base and 10 feet high, built from material dug out of a ditch on the inside. This ditch was 20 feet deep and 33 feet wide. Its excavator, Geoffrey Wainwright, has estimated that its construction would have taken 900,000 man hours — which sounds enormous though 250 people could manage that in a year. There were entrances on opposite sides, the lower being close to the River Avon. The diameter, east to west, is 1,720 feet crest to crest on the bank. Recent research has shown that the site was occupied from about 3200 BC and the earthwork constructed about 2550 BC. A strip of land beside the embankment was excavated in

38

Durrington Walls : required nearly a million man-hours of work

1966-68 and revealed the remains of two circular timber structures. The northern one may have been a round thatched building about 48 feet across with a roof raised in the centre to let in light and air. It was built about 2450 BC. In the southern circle there were the remains of two successive buildings of timber, but more probably it had a ring-shaped roof sloping inwards like a football stadium enclosing an open space with a circle of posts. The later building had six circles of posts. Its outer circle was 128 feet in diameter and was probably roofed with an opening at the centre, as seems to have been the case at Woodhenge. All these complicated monuments must be regarded as part of the Stonehenge religious centre. SOIL AND CULTIVATION: Chalk; bank partly grassed, interior and rest of bank ploughed. NEARBY LISTED SITES, PLACES OF INTEREST, REFRESHMENTS: See under Stonehenge.

East Kennett Long Barrow East Kennett, near Marlborough. Sheet 173, grid reference 116669. Late Neolithic chambered long barrow, about 3500 to 2500 BC. ACCESS RIGHTS: None; it is private land, but the barrow is so big that it is clearly visible from the lane that climbs out of East Kennett to the downs. *East Kennett is five miles west of Marlborough, a mile south of the A4, and you can park by the church. Walk to the farmhouse, the last building on the hilly side of the village, to ask for permission to walk up to the barrow. If this is given you turn sharp left inside the gate, as far as the boundary, and it is then an easy walk up the gallops to the tree-covered mound.* ARCHAEOLOGY: The largest long barrow in Britain, being 350 feet long by 100 feet wide, and 20 feet high. The sarsens of its burial chambers protrude at the south-east end. It is a wedge-shaped mound orientated north-west to south-east. Unexcavated and almost certainly intact, this great mound will be passed on for future generations to explore. It almost certainly has burial chambers that are as impressive as those of West Kennett, and possibly bigger as much more of the mound

East Kennett Long Barrow : keeps its secrets

survives at East Kennett. These would have been sealed with stones after several centuries of use. Side ditches show as lines of darker grass. The barrow stands on an exposed spur at 600 feet, with magnificent views in all directions and an especially fine one of Silbury Hill. SOIL AND CULTIVATION: Chalk; the mound is tree-covered. NEARBY LISTED SITES: West Kennett Long Barrow, Kennett Stone Avenue, Falkner's Circle, Silbury Hill, The Sanctuary, Overton Hill, Lockeridge Dene, Wansdyke. OTHER PLACES OF INTEREST, AND REFRESHMENTS: See under Silbury Hill.

Falkner's Circle opposite Kennett Stone Avenue, near Avebury. Sheet 173, grid reference 108693, though it is not marked by the Ordnance Survey. Early Bronze Age stone circle, about 2500 to 2000 BC. ACCESS RIGHTS: None; although it lies just inside the National Trust's Avebury estate this is leased farmland without provision for access, but the one remaining stone is visible from the road. *Turn off the A4 at West Kennett, five miles west of Marlborough, on the B4003 to Avebury. Park in half a mile at the south end of the preserved section of the Kennett Stone Avenue. The stone of Falkner's Circle is in the arable field opposite, in about a quarter of a mile, to the left of the hedgerow at the bend in the field.* ARCHAEOLOGY: An outlying stone circle to the Avebury complex has to be significant, even though it is sadly reduced to one stone. Nothing more has been standing since 1840, but before that there were two fallen stones as well, and nine socket-holes showed the location of the rest of the stones in the circle. These should be taken into account in any astronomical theories concerning Avebury, and perhaps eventually the National Trust may restore a right of access and show the positions of the lost stones with concrete markers. SOIL AND CULTIVATION: Chalk, ploughed to edge of stone. NEARBY LISTED SITES: Kennett Stone Avenue, Avebury, Silbury Hill, West Kennett Long Barrow, The Polissoir, The Sanctuary, Overton Hill. OTHER PLACES OF INTEREST, AND REFRESHMENTS: See under Avebury.

Figsbury Ring Winterbourne, near Salisbury. Sheet 184, grid reference 188338. Iron Age hill-fort, about 250 BC. ACCESS RIGHTS: National Trust land, freely open. *Four miles east of Salisbury on the north side of the A30, the Andover road. Signposted from the cluster of buildings at the dip in the hills. There is a large grassed car park at the end of a short track. The stile and path to Figsbury is to the left of a "Danger Keep Out" notice which refers to the adjoining Porton Downs military lands.* ARCHAEOLOGY: Figsbury stands conspicuously on the rounded chalk down about 500 feet above sea level. The top is level except on the western side where the entrenchment is carried down below the crest of the hill. It consists of a rampart with an outer ditch, enclosing 16 acres, but inside there is an unusual feature — a wide inner quarry ditch. It is concentric with the rampart but without any bank of its own. Excavation in 1924 showed that this was probably cut to provide additional chalk on one of the two occasions when the rampart was heightened. There are two original entrances through the rampart and corresponding causeways across the inner ditch, on the eastern and western sides. Outside the former are traces of a bank and ditch that once formed a horn-work or outer defence. There is now a wide gap in the rampart on the southern side but this is not an original feature. Stukeley does not show the gap in 1723 but Colt-Hoare in 1810 does. Apparently it was made between these years. Figsbury Ring was bought by the National Trust in 1930. SOIL AND

Figsbury Ring : rebuilt with chalk from an inner quarry ditch

CULTIVATION: Chalk; grassland — disappointing as the level ground has been sprayed with fertilizers, killing the orchids and rare flowers, but it is now the Trust's practice to prevent any repetition, to enable the gradual re-instatement of downland flora from the banks. NEARBY LISTED SITES: Stock Bottom, Old Sarum, Gallows Barrow, Milston Down. OTHER PLACES OF INTEREST, AND REFRESHMENTS: See under Old Sarum.

Fosbury Camp Vernham Dean, near Hungerford. Sheet 174, grid reference 320565. Iron Age hill-fort, about 150 BC. ACCESS RIGHTS: Public path crosses the northern side. *Turn off the A338 between East Grafton and Shalbourne on to the hills and to Oxenwood and Fosbury. Park at Fosbury and walk south from the centre of the hamlet, along the road to Fosbury Farm, in two thirds of a mile, where you turn left and walk into Oakhill Wood. Here, in half a mile or so, the path comes out of the trees into the fort and then follows the edge of the wood.* ARCHAEOLOGY: Double banked hill-fort, with an entrance to the east. One of the larger Wiltshire forts, enclosing 24 acres. SOIL AND CULTIVA-TION: Chalk; grass. NEARBY LISTED SITE: Tidcombe Down Long Barrow. OTHER PLACES OF INTEREST, AND REFRESHMENTS: See under Tidcombe Down Long Barrow.

Gallows Barrow Figheldean, near Amesbury. Sheet 184, grid reference 156480. Early Bronze Age oval barrow, about 2400 BC. ACCESS RIGHTS: Visible from public roads to the south. *Off the road north from Figheldean to Netheravon Airfield on the opposite side of the valley from the A345 and half a mile north of Figheldean, behind the thatched house beside the drive to New Farm Buildings. You can look down on it from the hill opposite.* ARCHAEOLOGY: Now accepted as a barrow type in their own right, oval mounds have gained new respecta-bility. They represent a transitional stage between long and round barrows. This one is about 75 feet long by 50 feet wide and six feet high, and has pro-duced Bronze Age sherds and a barbed and tanged flint arrowhead. The gallows connection dates back to at least the 17th century. Sarsen stones for Stonehenge were brought down this valley from the Marlborough Downs, a mishap leading to one of them ending up at the bottom of the River Avon in Figheldean. SOIL AND CULTIVATION: Chalk; downland. NEARBY LISTED SITES: Sidbury Hill, Casterley Camp, Figsbury Ring, Milston

41

Down. OTHER PLACES OF INTEREST, AND REFRESHMENTS: See under Vespasian's Camp.

Giant's Cave Luckington, near Malmesbury. Sheet 173, grid reference 821829. Late Neolithic chambered long barrow, about 3500 to 2500 BC. ACCESS RIGHTS: Clearly visible, between two roads at a junction, but to walk over the barrow ask permission of Mr M. Windell at Allengrove Farm, half a mile to the north. *Turn off the B4040 half a mile south of Luckington, towards Great Badminton. In half a mile, at the edge of Badminton Park, the barrow is on the right, 200 yards along the road to "Cherry Orchard".* ARCHAEOLOGY: Barrow 135 feet long by 85 feet wide orientated north-west to south-east, about ten feet high, containing at least five chambers of limestone blocks along the sides. The stones of these can still be traced and the remains of 20 burials have been found though there must have been many more. John Aubrey wrote in *Monumenta Britannica:* "It is long and some oaks and other boscage (scrub) cover it. Here were accidentally discovered since the year 1646, certain small caves, about five or six in number. They were about four foot in height and seven or eight feet long; being floored, lined and coursed with great plank-stones, which are plentiful hereabout. I saw them 1659." Since then the ends of the barrow have been ripped out for road-making stone. Some of the damage was done in the 1880s and an 80-year-old ex-council roadman at Luckington used to have a skull from the mound as a memento. The inner chambers were excavated 1960-62, with finds at Devizes Museum. One side stone to a chamber is still visible, about 14 feet long. There was a V-shaped courtyard at the east end, and all round a retaining wall of tiny stones which in places the farmer, Mr M. Windell, has covered with brushwood clippings to protect them from the hooves of the cows. Giant's Cave lies in an area rich with gigantic associations — Hercules Hill to the south-west, and Tickle Conner's Tump outside Badminton House which the Duchess of Beaufort had excavated in the 1950s. Its skeleton was 6 feet 8 inches to 7 feet tall, and her grace insisted that after the scientific tests he was reburied in his grave. But the puzzle about Giant's Cave is that its big bodies would have been pushed into the chambers through openings only 13 to 15 inches wide.

Grey Wethers or Sarsen Stones Fyfield Down, near Marlborough. Sheet 173, grid reference 140704. Natural deposits of sarsen boulders, from which the megalithic builders took their stone. ACCESS RIGHTS: The Valley of Stones lies within the Fyfield Down National Nature Reserve, which is open freely though you are asked to keep to the paths. *Park in Fyfield village, on A4 two miles west of Marlborough. Leave your car off the main road, by barn on side road to church. Opposite there is a farm road signposted uphill to Temple Bottom. In half a mile there is a farm and from here a path leads downhill to a gate. Through the gate you turn left, into the nature reserve, and follow the line of the hedge. In half a mile you come to a valley where countless thousands of these huge sarsen stones are to be seen, a quite amazing sight.* ARCHAEOLOGY: These sarsen stones are the remnants of a siliceous duricrust layer which formed on an eocene surface in the early tertiary times some 70 million years ago. Climatic conditions were warm and wet. Some of the roots that penetrated the sarsen beds from above were palms, leaving holes which can still be seen, generally on one side of the stones. The sarsen layer in this region, when it had hardened, must have capped the downs at 700 to 800 feet before the

Grey Wethers : the valley floor is strewn with sarsens

surface was deformed by the same movements of the earth's crust which formed the European Alps 30 million years ago. This disturbance caused the break-up of the layer and the gradual transportation of most of the stones down the slope to their present positions below their original bed. SOIL AND CULTIVATION: Chalk, unimproved downland sheep pastures. NEARBY LISTED SITES: The Polissoir, Devil's Den, Piggledene. OTHER PLACES OF INTEREST, AND REFRESHMENTS: See under Silbury Hill.

Grim's Ditch Swayne's Firs, near Salisbury. Sheet 184, grid reference 070222. Late Bronze Age tribal boundary, about 1200 BC. ACCESS RIGHTS: Visible beside road. *Take the A354 Salisbury to Blandford road four miles on to the downs above Coombe Bissett. Here, less than a mile before the start of the dual carriageway, is a sign "Knighton Estate, Crouchestone Down Farm" on the north side of the road. Immediately opposite is a small layby beside the "Hampshire" county sign. In the paddock on the Wiltshire side of the layby is a section of double bank with a ditch between. Pine trees grow on it. This is one of the best intact sections of Grim's Ditch. It is in private ownership, though application at Swayne's Firs Farm usually results in permission to walk along the course of the ditch.* ARCHAEOLOGY: Grim's Ditch is a continuous earthwork. It is a ditch between two banks that wanders up hill and down dale across the eastern part of Cranborne Chase. In length it is about 14 miles and its usual width is from 50 to 60 feet, from outside to outside of the banks. Where it is well preserved the superficial bottom of the ditch is five to six feet below the higher bank. It turns and twists in a manner now unintelligible. Some sections are completely obliterated by the plough. Basically the ditch runs from Middle Chase Farm to Down Barn, about two and a half miles west of Clearbury Ring. The ditch is of great antiquity, and was probably the late Bronze Age border between two tribes. It is still a county boundary. Though it is too

Grim's Ditch : boundary running for miles

small to have been defensive it could have served as the ranch boundary of a cattle range. SOIL AND CULTIVATION: Chalk; some grassland or over-grown but mostly ploughed. NEARBY LISTED SITES: Ackling Dyke, Wudu-Burh, Clearbury Ring. OTHER PLACES OF INTEREST: Coombe Bisset and Broad Chalke both have splendid churches. The great Romano-British earthwork in the area is the massive defence against the Saxons, Bokerley Ditch beside the A354 three miles west, at the ''Dorset'' sign. It is described in the author's ''Exploring Ancient Dorset'' (also from Dorset Publishing Company). REFRESHMENTS: There are many wayside inns along this road.

Hamshill Ditches Barford St Martin, near Wilton. Sheet 184, grid reference 058332. Romano-British enclosures and field system, about 100 to 450 AD. ACCESS RIGHTS: The general area is crossed by public track-ways. *Turn off the A30 beside its junction with the B3089 at Barford St Martin, five miles west of Salisbury. Take the road alongside the Green Dragon Inn, and drive under the railway arch. Follow this lane for nearly a mile, to a double bend. Park at the second corner. Straight ahead there is a fenced trackway with a ''Public Footpath'' sign, beside a milestone ''VI miles from Sarum 1759''. The Celtic field system is visible to the right of the track. The ditches are in half a mile, at the end of the area of rough downland between the field and the wood. In the field itself they have been ploughed out.* ARCHAEOLOGY: The two main features are fragmentary round enclosures. They are evidently of the spectacle type and are connected by a ditch, cut for communication between them. Each side of the causeway is a ditch but it is broken in the middle of the north side, probably for access to dwelling areas. Excavation has turned up many Romano-British artefacts and there can be no doubt that Hamshill was the site of an extensive native community throughout Roman times. Roman coins and carved stone have been found in the wood. The spectacle enclosures were most likely used for the penning of livestock. SOIL AND CULTIVATION: Chalk; in variety of uses, arable, open downland, and wooded. NEARBY LISTED SITES: Wick Ball Camp, Chiselbury Camp. OTHER PLACES OF INTEREST: Barford St Martin is a charming village with a beautiful 13th century church. There is a pre-Reformation preaching cross. Do not miss the curious portrait in stone of a woman in quilted garments kneeling by a pot piled high with loaves. There is a brass of Alice Walker on her death bed surrounded by her 11 children. Wilton, sometime Saxon capital of Wessex, has one of the treasure houses of England. Wilton House, confiscated from nuns, was embellished by Inigo Jones and is open to the public. It also has lovely gardens. REFRESHMENTS: Good bar meals at the Green Dragon, Barford St Martin.

Kennett Stone Avenue Avebury, near Marlborough. Sheet 173, grid reference 105695. Early Bronze Age stone row, about 2500 to 2000 BC. ACCESS RIGHTS: Surviving part National Trust land, in the guardianship of the Department of the Environment, open freely. *Turn north from the A4 at Beckhampton roundabout, seven miles west of Marlborough, on the A36 towards Swindon. Leave your car in the Avebury car park, in a mile on your left as you approach the earthwork. Walk along the road towards the earthwork and then turn right, into the B4003. This road follows the Kennett Stone Avenue and cuts through it at one point. There is a gate at the corner and you can walk between the two rows of stones and markers.* ARCHAEOLOGY: The stones are 80 feet apart, in two lines 50 feet wide. Only the northern half mile remains in recognisable form, and its lost stones are marked with concrete. Sinuously it enters the Avebury circle and originally there was a similar kink where it joined another stone circle at its now destroyed opposite end, the Sanctuary on Overton Hill. The course of the stones from Avebury to West Kennett and Overton Hill, ''a kind of solemn walk'' of a mile and a half, was sketched by John Aubrey in his 17th century *Monumenta Britannica* but only odd stones now survive in the southern two thirds. The Kennett Stone Avenue must date from the second half of Avebury's existence, as chalk blocks from the bottom of its ditch were used to pack the stones into the ground. Burials beside four of the stone holes at the Overton Hill end were accompanied by

Kennett Stone Avenue : impressive as it approaches Avebury

45

Kennett Stone Avenue : Stukeley's 1724 views of its Avebury end and the better preserved mid-section

the pottery of the Beaker people, immigrants from Holland and the Rhine who brought the Bronze Age to Britain and adopted its megalithic traditions. SOIL AND CULTIVATION: Chalk, grassland. NEARBY LISTED SITES: Avebury, Falkner's Circle, The Sanctuary, Overton Hill, West Kennett Long Barrow, Silbury Hill, Beckhampton Long Barrow, Adam and Eve Stones, The Polissoir. OTHER PLACES OF INTEREST, AND REFRESHMENTS: See under Avebury.

Knap Hill Pewsey Downs, near Pewsey. Sheet 173, grid reference 122637 Neolithic causewayed camp, about 4000 to 2500 BC. ACCESS RIGHTS: In the Pewsey Downs National Nature Reserve, open freely. *Turn off the A345 at Pewsey, north-west to Wilcot Green and cross the Kennet and Avon Canal. Keep on this road to Alton Priors, where you turn right at the crossroads and drive uphill on to the downs. Park almost at the top, in the layby on your left. Walk uphill along the road for about 200 yards, passing two round barrows on each side of the road. You then turn right, just after the largest barrow, along a wide cattle drove. This leads to Knap Hill, the hill in profile on your left. From the end of the drove a footpath leads off to the left, up the hill.* ARCHAEOLOGY: Knap Hill is one of the best preserved Neolithic settlements in Britain, the causewayed gaps in the bank about 18 feet wide, being clearly visible from the road. It encloses four acres. Pottery, now in Devizes Museum, was found in the ditch in 1908, with fragments of antler picks, a human jawbone, flint flakes, and chips of sarsen stone. An Iron Age farmstead of half an acre was tacked on to the already ancient Neolithic earthwork, on the east side, early in the 1st century AD. SOIL AND CULTIVATION: Chalk; open downland. NEARBY LISTED SITES: Adam's Grave, Wansdyke, Swanborough Tump. OTHER PLACES OF INTEREST, AND REFRESHMENTS: See under Adam's Grave.

Knap Hill : perfectly preserved settlement of the first farmers

47

Lanhill Long Barrow Barrow Hill, near Chippenham. Sheet 173, grid reference 877747. Late Neolithic chambered long barrow, about 3500 to 2500 BC. ACCESS RIGHTS: Visible from road and public footpath which crosses the field less than a hundred yards from the Chippenham side of the barrow. *Two miles west of Chippenham on the south side of the A420, between the B4039 Chipping Sodbury turn off and that to Kington St.Michael, beside a wide verge. There is a paddock gate into the field, opposite a farm drive.* ARCHAE-OLOGY: Orientated west to east with a mound 190 feet long by 90 feet wide and six feet high, and a dummy portal 35 feet from the higher end. The ends of the barrow were destroyed in the 1950s. There are two chambers, covered, on the north side and an impressive corbelled chamber visible on the south edge, splendidly restored. Some 20 bodies have been found and those in one chamber were from the same family. Formerly known as Hubbaslow, "low" being the Danish word for barrow. SOIL AND CULTI-VATION: Limestone; grassed. NEARBY LISTED SITES: Lugbury, Three Shire Stones. OTHER PLACES OF INTEREST: Corsham Court, on the A4 west of Chippenham, of 1582 in Capability Brown parkland. Open all year on Sunday, Wednesday and Thursday, and Tuesday and Saturday as well from June to September. REFRESHMENTS: In Corsham or Chippenham.

Lanhill Long Barrow : the burial chamber

Liddington Castle Liddington, near Swindon. Sheet 174, grid reference 209797. Iron Age hill-fort, about 250 BC. ACCESS RIGHTS: The fort is a quarter of a mile beyond the official line of a bridleway, but there has been past public access, including the erection of a plaque to Alfred Williams the poet, by courtesy of the owner. *Turn off the A419 Swindon to Hungerford road on the side of the hill a third of a mile south of its flyover across the M4. There is a staggered crossroads and you park near this junction: take the Chiseldon and Marlborough turn. On the left in 100 yards you can park up the bypassed stub-end of old lane. At the junction, opposite the barn, a bridleway runs on the field side of the left-hand, eastern, main road hedge for 250 yards in the Hungerford direction. Liddington Hill is on the other side of the road. Opposite the stile, on the other side of the road,*

there is a bridleway, part of the Ridgeway path, which climbs to the top.
ARCHAEOLOGY: Liddington Castle is a recent title — it was known as
Badbury to Aubrey, Stukeley and the other early antiquaries. Badbury is
still the name of the hamlet at its foot. Double banked with a ditch between
and an entrance at the south-east. Exposed portions of the main bank show
that sarsen stones were used to face the inner rampart. The bank still rises
up to ten feet above the interior. About eight acres are enclosed. Iron Age
A-period finds from the fort, including saddle querns, spindle worls, loom
weights and a bronze awl, are in the A.D. Passmore collection at the Ash-
molean Museum in Oxford. A pagan Saxon iron spearhead was also found
on the hill. The plateau is at 900 feet and has superb views in all directions.
"Liddington Hill, the hill beloved by Richard Jefferies and Alfred Will-
iams" reads the plaque on the Ordnance Survey's pillar. SOIL AND CUL-
TIVATION: Chalk; open downland. NEARBY LISTED SITES: Liddington
Long Barrow, Aldbourne Four Barrows, Upper Upham Field System,
Coate Stone Circle, Membury Fort, Barbury Castle. OTHER PLACES OF
INTEREST, AND REFRESHMENTS: See under Aldbourne Four Barrows.

Liddington Long Barrow Liddington, near Swindon. Sheet 174, grid reference 225798. Neolithic chambered long barrow, about 3500 to 2500 BC.
ACCESS RIGHTS: Crossed by public bridleway. *Turn off the A419 Swindon to
Hungerford road on the side of the hill a third of a mile south of its flyover across the
M4, at a staggered crossroads. Opposite the barn, a bridleway runs on the field side of
the left-hand, eastern, main road hedge for about a third of a mile in the Hungerford
direction and then swings away from the main road to follow the left-hand side of the
fence along a low ridge. In a further third of a mile you pass the barrow on the top of the
rise at the side of the field.* ARCHAEOLOGY: Medium sized long barrow, 150
feet long by 40 feet wide and four feet high. Sarsens of the burial chambers
protrude from the mound. Used since ancient times as a landmark, the
parish boundary being set along its north-west to south-east alignment.
Three skeletons were found in 1890 during the erection of a farm fence,
and another subsequently. SOIL AND CULTIVATION: Chalk; grassland.
NEARBY LISTED SITES: Liddington Castle, Coate Stone Circle, Aldbourne Four Barrows, Upper Upham Field System, Barbury Castle,
Membury Fort. PLACES OF INTEREST, AND REFRESHMENTS: See
under Aldbourne Four Barrows.

Littlecote Roman Mosaic Littlecote Park, Chilton Foliat, near Hungerford. Sheet 174, grid reference 299707. Roman mosaic floor, about 150
AD. ACCESS RIGHTS: Open to public but at present covered in winter, re-
opened weekends from Easter and then weekdays July to September. *Turn
off A419 Hungerford to Swindon road a mile outside Hungerford, just east of Chilton
Foliat. Littlecote House is clearly signposted. The Roman villa is in the grounds
beyond the house, beside the Kennet meadows.* ARCHAEOLOGY: The finest
Roman mosaic floor ever unearthed in Britain, the restoration of which was
one of the triumphs of archaeology in the 1970s. It had been unearthed in
1723 but was afterwards covered and the site lost. The pavement was
"believed subsequently destroyed" according to the Victoria County
History. Its location was rediscovered in the early 1970s and the present re-
paired floor — 41 feet by 28 feet of artistic wonderment — is due to the fact
that William George, the steward who found the pavement, made painstaking coloured drawings showing the precise design of the figures.

Littlecote : floor of the Orphic temple, the finest mosaic in Britain

These, coupled with the foresight and funds of D.W. Wills of the tobacco family who owns the house, enabled archaeologists to attempt restoration to the present level of perfection. The central medallion of the inner chamber is a representation of Orpheus and the four quadrant ends contain a rapidly moving beast and dancing female figure. There are also dolphins and sea creatures. This was the religious room or temple serving the house, and also served as a precinct to its bathroom. It can be closely dated to 360 AD by the miraculous chance of three coins having been lost in its core. This was the period of the pagan revival and the reign of Julian Apostate, but this fine floor was only to be in use for ten years. Rooms to the south-west of the villa are the foundations of a *mansio* or inn of about 160 AD. It was a civil service lodging house, for travellers along the Roman road and the administrators of an associated corn-tax depot. As a taxation station it would certainly have had its own fort, which has yet to be discovered. Littlecote's other finds include the only Roman oak brewing vat to be found in Britain. A remarkable feature of the main villa is that its bath-house appears to have been re-used in the 11th century, and from then until 1400 there was a mediaeval village across the nine acre Roman site. It is being excavated with dedication and enthusiasm by Bryn Walters who has established the Littlecote Roman Research Trust, to ensure the future of the work now that its costs have escalated beyond the means of the estate. He hopes to do more than merely house the mosaic under a modern roof, visualising a full-scale replica villa rising from the meadows. As a mark of the painstaking seriousness of the venture the team has already dug out the actual Roman course of the Kennet and diverted the river back into it. They have discovered a total of 33 villas in this part of Wiltshire, where before only a handful were known. Four are now known on the Littlecote estate alone, and the Trust has to tackle that at Rudge before the onset of deep ploughing. All this work will become increasingly costly, but it is providing knowledge in a spectacular form, and its success depends upon all

50

who cherish ancient Wiltshire. Donations both large and small will be appreciated by the Littlecote Roman Research Trust at the Coach House, Littlecote, Hungerford. SOIL AND CULTIVATION: Gravel; grassland. NEARBY LISTED SITES: Aldbourne Four Barrows, Cunetione, Upper Upham Field System, Membury Fort. OTHER PLACES OF INTEREST: Littlecote House, Elizabethan Manor, home of Wild Will Darrel who was tried for murder in one of the most sensational cases in British history. Acquitted against all the evidence but died in a riding accident soon afterwards. Hungerford is a small picturesque town, mainly devoted to the antique trade. REFRESHMENTS: Ample good inns at Hungerford.

Lockeridge Dene Lockeridge, near Marlborough. Sheet 173, grid reference 144674. Natural sarsen stones. ACCESS RIGHTS: National Trust land, always open. *Park by the green at the west end of Lockeridge village. A field of sarsens lies on the valley floor, with thatched cottages spread around it. There is a larger field of sarsens, also owned by the National Trust, a little further up the valley — just after the far cottage.* ARCHAEOLOGY: Important deposit of Grey Wethers, so called from their resemblance to sheep. These sarsen or sandstone boulders are fragments of a former capping to the chalk in remote times. The roots of palm trees, which then grew from this, caused the holes in the stones. The sarsens were used by the megalithic builders of the Neolithic and Bronze Age periods. This particular deposit is an outlier from the main area of the higher downs, and has the virtue of being the most accessible. The cluster of cottages is highly attractive, being set around the deposits of sarsens. This ground was used as common land by the cottagers. SOIL AND CULTIVATION: Chalk; paddock and pasture. NEARBY LISTED SITES: Piggledene, Grey Wethers, Devil's Den, Martinsell Hill, Wansdyke, East Kennett Long Barrow, The Sanctuary, Overton Hill. OTHER PLACES OF INTEREST, AND REFRESHMENTS: See under Silbury Hill

Lockeridge Dene : cottages look out on to a field of sarsens

51

Lugbury Nettleton, near Castle Combe. Sheet 173, grid reference 831786. Late Neolithic chambered long barrow, about 3500 to 2500 BC. ACCESS RIGHTS: Two public bridleways pass the south and west sides. *Off the Fosse Way half a mile south of its Ship Inn crossroads with the B4039. There is a leg of wood on the west side of the Fosse at the top of the southern side of the valley. A bridleway follows the trees for a quarter of a mile and passes the barrow, which is clearly visible.* ARCHAEOLOGY: Though reduced in height by ploughing the mound is 200 feet long by 80 feet wide and six feet high. There are the stones of a false entrance at the east end. Two uprights six and seven feet high have a capstone 12 feet long by five feet high resting against them. Four limestone burial chambers along the south side, now covered, were excavated by Colt Hoare and G.P. Scrope in 1825 and 1855, revealing one empty chamber and 31 skeletons in the rest. All were long-headed, having a length more than one-fifth greater than the width. SOIL AND CULTIVATION: Limestone; ploughed to edge in barley. NEARBY LISTED SITES: Giant's Cave, Lanhill Long Barrow, Three Shire Stones. OTHER PLACES OF INTEREST: Castle Combe is regarded by many as the prettiest village in England, a view frequently endorsed by the film companies who have even converted its stream-side range of stone-roofed Cotswold cottages into a functioning wharf. REFRESHMENTS: Castle Combe, where the Manor is an hotel.

Lugbury : false entrance to a mound that is mostly gone

Martinsell Hill Oare, near Pewsey. Sheet 173, grid reference 176641. Iron Age hill-fort, about 50 BC. ACCESS RIGHTS: Public paths follow the north and west ramparts. *Turn off the A345 at the top of the hill a mile north of Oare, where a track is signposted eastwards to "Martinsell". Just along this track there is a natural car park. Leave car here and climb Oare Hill, after passing through a wooden gate. The ascent to the hill-fort is an easy stroll of less than a mile, and the path follows the edge of the wood.* ARCHAEOLOGY: One of the largest hill-forts in Wiltshire in terms of area, enclosing 34 acres, but it is only single banked. Apparently connected with a ditch and bank that led to a settlement on

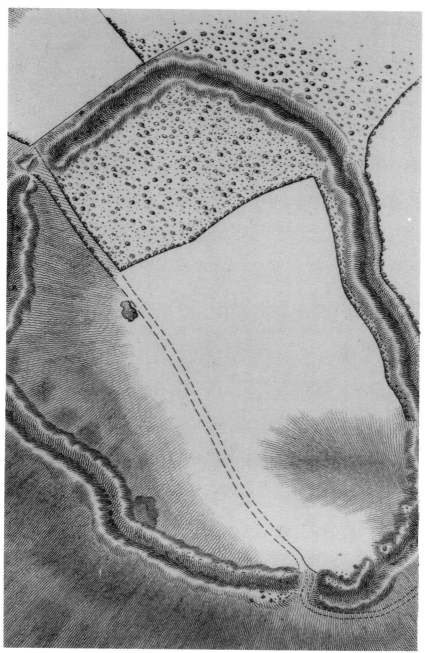

Membury Fort : plan from Colt Hoare's *Ancient Wiltshire,* 1819 volume, showing the public path across the centre

Huish Hill. There is a difficulty in regarding this as a pastoral enclosure for that settlement, as the entrance to the fort is in the wrong place — the north-east corner. There is also a promontory fort on the west end of the spur, above Oare and crossed by a public path, which is known as the Giant's Grave. Martinsell Hill was known as "Maetelmes burh" in 940 AD. Contents of a large Roman military rubbish pit, excavated in 1907, are in Devizes Museum. Set in a most beautiful part of the Wiltshire Downs, with views that are superb on a clear summer day. SOIL AND CULTIVATION: Chalk; banks downland, interior ploughed and under cereals. NEARBY LISTED SITES: Lockeridge Dene, Cunetione. OTHER PLACES OF INTEREST: Pewsey, small market town with inns and church which although vandalised by the Victorian restorers is still worth a visit. Public towpath along the Kennet and Avon Canal. REFRESHMENTS: Cross the canal at Bridge Wharf, near Pewsey. Friendly service and bar snacks and meals available at the French Horn and Barge Inn on the other side of the road.

Membury Fort Whittonditch, Ramsbury, near Hungerford. Sheet 174, grid reference 302752. Iron Age hill-fort, about 75 BC. ACCESS RIGHTS: Public footpath crosses the banks and runs through the centre of the fort. *Turn off the A419 Swindon to Hungerford road at Whittonditch, opposite the second turn to Ramsbury. It is signposted "Membury". Drive up the valley for a mile and a half and turn left opposite a cottage and an old chapel. The lane is signed "Marridge Hill 1". In a quarter of a mile the road bends to climb the hill. Park and walk straight ahead along the farm track towards the tall mast at the top of the valley. At the trees and buildings in half a mile you turn sharply right and follow the line of trees up the slope. Outside the fort the path swings left and then right before entering the earthworks. You can continue straight ahead across the flat top. The trees on the other side are in Berkshire.* ARCHAEOLOGY: Double banked with a ditch between, tree covered and known as Walls Copse, enclosing 34 acres. The ground is scattered with the burnt flints from prehistoric grain-drying ovens, indicating a substantial settlement. SOIL AND CULTIVATION: Chalk; banks wooded, interior ploughed and under cereals. NEARBY LISTED SITES: Aldbourne Four Barrows, Liddington Long Barrow, Upper Upham Field System, Littlecote Roman Mosaic. OTHER PLACES OF INTEREST: Ashdown House, National Trust property between Lambourn and Ashdown. Littlecote House, near Hungerford. REFRESHMENTS: The Crown and Anchor and the Bell at Ramsbury, a long town street with much half-timbering and thatch.

Middle Hill Norton Bavant, near Warminster. Sheet 184, grid reference 910448. Cultivation terraces, probably Iron Age about 50 BC. ACCESS RIGHTS: Public track runs beside them at the foot of the slope. *Turn off the A36 between Warminster and Heytesbury. Two miles east from Warminster there is a lane marked "North Farm" with a no through road sign, opposite a bus stop. Turn along, over the railway line. In half a mile, after a cottage and at the top of the slope, you come to a sharp bend to the right. Park here, off the road at the corner. The lynchets are to the left of the dirt track that continues straight ahead.* ARCHAEOLOGY: Whatever their date may be, these are some of the finest strip lynchets to be seen anywhere, and they still do their job of preventing soil loss by erosion. SOIL AND CULTIVATION: Chalk; slopes grass, terraces ploughed. NEARBY LISTED SITES: Scratchbury Hill, Battlesbury Hill, Cley Hill, Westbury White Horse, Bratton Castle. OTHER PLACES OF INTEREST, AND REFRESHMENTS: See under Scratchbury Hill.

Milston Down Bulford Camp, near Amesbury. Sheet 184, grid reference 217463. Neolithic long barrows, about 4000 to 3000 BC. ACCESS RIGHTS: Visible beside public road. *Midway between Bulford Camp and Tidworth Garrison, on the north side of the road that connects the two establishments. Turn off the A3028 to Bulford, or from the A338 at Tidworth. Situated two miles from each base, on the north side of the road just west of The Belt, a line of woods.* ARCHAEOLOGY: It is unusual to find two long barrows so close together. These are orientated east to west, only yards apart, with one 160 feet long by seven feet high and the other 90 feet long by four feet high. As is often the case their presence seems to have attracted a continuation of burial practice, and the area on both sides of the road is studded with numerous later Bronze Age round barrows, as well as a ranch boundary known as the Devil's Ditch. SOIL AND CULTIVATION: Chalk; mounds grass ploughed to edge. NEARBY LISTED SITES: Gallows Barrow, Figsbury Ring. OTHER PLACES OF INTEREST, AND REFRESHMENTS: See under Sidbury Hill.

Normanton Down Wilsford, near Amesbury. Sheet 184, grid reference 116413. Bronze Age barrow cemetery, about 2100 to 1500 BC. ACCESS RIGHTS: Green lane, a public byway, goes through the centre of the cemetery, across the edge of a disc barrow, and a footpath is signposted from it. *Two-thirds of a mile south from Stonehenge a trackway crosses the A303, to the west of the monument. Half a mile along this track the cemetery is clearly visible, on both sides of the byway.* ARCHAEOLOGY: The major Stonehenge barrow group, strung along the flat top of the southern down. The mounds, described as the finest collection in Britain, are impressive but the setting is a disappointing prairie of barley. Excavations have revealed urns and cremations, rich with grave goods including faience beads from Egypt, Kimmeridge shale from Dorset, and amber from the North Sea coast. One skeleton had a breast-plate lozenge of gold and a dagger inlaid with the metal, as well as a bronze axe, mace and shield. This was the burial beneath Bush Barrow, the closest big mound to the left of the path. The temptation must be to consider this the burial ground of the greatest of the Wessex chiefs, the builders of Stonehenge. The mounds are of many types, ranging from the low disc mound set in flat ground with a distance ditch and bank, to large bell-shaped mounds and the bowl barrows which are the standard prehistoric burial mound, though at Normanton there was nothing ordinary about their contents. Finds, including a grape-shaped cup, in Devizes Museum. SOIL AND CULTIVATION: Chalk; mounds, ploughed to the edge. NEARBY LISTED SITES, PLACES OF INTEREST, REFRESHMENTS: See under Stonehenge.

Normanton Down : the Bush Barrow, right, contained a chieftain's gold

Old Sarum Salisbury. Sheet 184, grid reference 137327. Iron Age hill-fort, about 100 BC, re-used in subsequent ages. ACCESS RIGHTS: In Department of Environment guardianship; outer earthworks open freely at all times, admission charge to the inner castle. *At the northern edge of Salisbury, signposted from the A345, Amesbury road. Car park inside the earthworks.* ARCHAEOLOGY: Old Sarum has had a far more interesting history than most of the hill-forts. It has been occupied by Iron Age man, Romans, Saxons, Danes and Normans. King Alfred ordered Leofric of Wiltshire to repair the castle and build another ditch defended by palisades. In 1003 it was captured and all the buildings burnt by Sweyn king of Denmark. The Norman kings frequently visited the castle and a cathedral, consecrated 1092, was built inside the west gate. The soldiers continued to occupy the castle for another 50 years before deciding to descend into the much warmer site in the valley. The castle and then the cathedral fell into disuse and ruin. Most of the facing stone, Tisbury greensand, was robbed for the building of the new city, leaving the exposed flint core of the walls on the hilltop. Stukeley described the site as impregnable to anything but death and hunger. Note especially the height of the ramparts which here exceed 100 feet, against the 50 feet maximum of most forts, though they would have been deepened by the Saxons and the Normans. SOIL AND CULTIVATION: Chalk; grassland, fouled by the practice of using it as a dogs' lavatory for the town. NEARBY LISTED SITES: Stock Bottom, Figsbury Ring, Stonehenge. OTHER PLACES OF INTEREST: Salisbury is one of the most beautiful cities in England with its great cathedral built by Bishop Poore in 1220. The spire, at 404 feet, is the tallest in the world. Mompesson House in the Close is open to the public. Salisbury Museum is a treasure house, as in fact are the churches of St Martin, St Thomas and St Edmund. To see Salisbury properly a full day should be put aside for the purpose. REFRESHMENTS: Ample choice in the city.

Old Sarum : Bishop Roger's palace, early 12th century, with the keep in the background

Old Sarum : the deepest ditch in Wiltshire

Old Sarum : foundations of the Norman cathedral

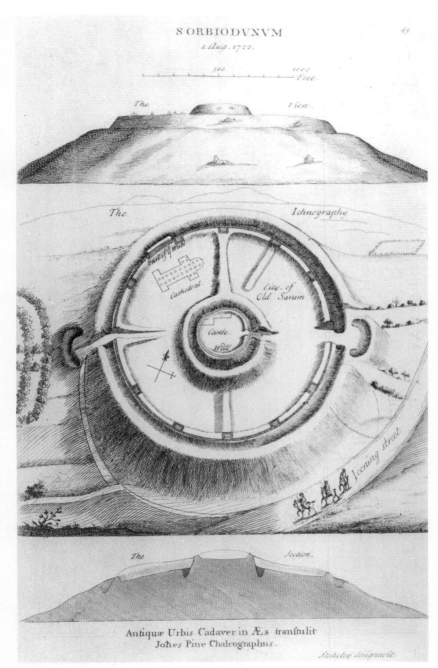

Old Sarum : William Stukeley's 1722 engraving

Oldbury Castle Cherhill, near Calne. Sheet 173, grid reference 050693. Iron Age hill fort, occupied at least from 300 to 100 BC. ACCESS RIGHTS: National Trust land, freely open, 138 acres on the 852 feet ridge being purchased in 1979. *To the south of the A4 midway between Calne and Silbury Hill. Park in Cherhill; laybys each side of the road at the Avebury end of the village. There is a track, signposted "Devizes", southwards from the main road at this end of the village, uphill to the large round barrow on the western summit and then left along the hilltop to the Monument and the National Trust land.* ARCHAEOLOGY: Triangular double-banked hill-fort enclosing 20 acres. The earthworks have been damaged by digging for flint, and chalk from these quarries was used in refurbishing the adjacent White Horse. This is on the northern slopes of the down, inside the National Trust land, and was cut by Dr Christopher Alsop of Calne in 1780. The views from the fort are outstanding. SOIL AND CULTIVATION: Chalk; unimproved open downland. NEARBY LISTED SITES: Beckhampton Roman Road, Wansdyke. OTHER PLACES OF INTEREST, AND REFRESHMENTS: See under Avebury.

Overton Hill Barrows West Kennett, near Marlborough. Sheet 173, grid reference 119683. Bronze Age burial mounds, about 2100 to 1500 BC. ACCESS RIGHTS: Visible from the public trackway along the hilltop. *Skyline barrow cemetery, on either side of the road five miles west of Marlborough, near the Ridgeway Cafe. Park on the north side of the road, on the wide verge of the Ridgeway next to the cafe car park.* ARCHAEOLOGY: The largest of the many scatterings of barrows on the downs above Avebury, prominently positioned. Known locally as Sevenbarrow Hill, its name — *Seofon beorgas* — appearing in a Saxon charter of 956, though the Ordnance Survey has unfortunately failed to pick it up. There are in fact a dozen barrows though only seven are prominent. Excavated by Sir Richard Colt Hoare, the 19th century antiquary who lived at Stourhead, with grave goods in Devizes Museum. Listed and described from south to north, as they are in a convenient line. *1.* Bowl barrow twelve feet high, which covered a crouched skeleton of a chieftain or warrior with bronze dagger and flat bronze axe, in a coffin hollowed out from a tree trunk. *2.* The next mound is no more; visible in William Stukeley's time it has since disappeared, though it does show faintly from the air. *3.* Twelve feet high bell barrow, but its formerly distinctive shape has now become the usual featureless rounded mound. It covered a primary cremation, the term 'primary' meaning that it was of the one which the mound was constructed to cover, accompanied with a "very rude little cup, scratched over with the usual British pattern". *4.* Another

Overton Hill : skyline barrow group, drawn by William Stukeley in the 1720s

59

Overton Hill : magnificent bell barrow, from Colt Hoare's *Ancient Wiltshire,* 1819

bell barrow, ten feet high, over a cremation. *5.* Small bowl barrow, only three feet high, squashed between the bell barrows on each side and apparently overlapping them, which contained a cremation and a bone pin. *6.* Bell barrow ten feet high, with a primary warrior cremation, buried with a bronze dagger. A secondary cremation was inserted into the barrow later and covered with sarsen stones. *7.* Eight feet high bowl barrow, contained a cremation. *8.* Tiny mound, only a foot high, excavated with no result. *9.* Another one foot mound. *10.* Three foot high mound, nothing known of its contents. *11.* One foot high mound containing ashes, burnt bones and damaged bronzework. *12.* Bowl barrow seven feet high with a main crema- tion at the centre and two secondary cremations inserted later near the top, one beneath an inverted coarse-ware urn. *13.* This barrow is away from the main group but it is worth the walk as it is one of the finest bell barrows in Wiltshire and a superb example of the sophisticated Wessex culture mounds. Walk northward along the Ridgeway for about three quarters of a mile. The barrow is about a quarter of a mile on the Avebury side of the track but visible from it. The mound is 85 feet in diameter and 12 feet high, encircled by a flat berm of untouched ground 27 feet wide, and then by a ditch, also concentric, which is 15 feet wide and two feet deep. As far as is known it is unexcavated. *14.* Another offshoot from the main group, this also justifies a short walk. It is well preserved disc barrow which is one of the rarer Wessex types. Turn westwards, towards Avebury, along the track that branches off the Ridgeway midway barrows 12 and 13. Follow it for about a quarter mile. The disc barrow is beside the farm track, on the right-hand side at the edge of the hill. Its centre mound or tump is 24 feet across and a foot high, which is the normal sort of size for this specialist type which appear to have been made for female burials. The flat area between the mound and the ditch is 27 feet in diameter. The ditch is 14 feet wide and a foot deep, encircled by a bank 18 feet wide and a foot high. Excavated without results. After you have wandered around these barrows you will have a clear idea of the basic types and spot many others as you walk or drive between the major monuments in the Avebury area. SOIL AND CULTIVATION: Chalk; grass, ploughed to edge. NEARBY LISTED SITES: The Sanctuary, The Polissoir, Kennett Stone Avenue, Falkner's Circle, East Kennett Long Barrow, West Kennett Long Barrow, Silbury Hill. OTHER PLACES OF INTEREST, AND REFRESHMENTS: See under Silbury Hill.

Piggledene Fyfield, near Marlborough. Sheet 173, grid reference 143686. Natural sarsen stones. ACCESS RIGHTS: National Trust land, always open. *Park in Fyfield village, on A4 two miles west of Marlborough. Leave your car off the main road, by barn on side road to church. Walk a third of a mile along the footway beside the A4, towards Avebury. Piggledene is the valley floor on the north side of the road, beside the "Fyfield ¼, Lockeridge ½" sign.* ARCHAEOLOGY: Of interest for its deposit of Grey Wethers, so called from their resemblance to sheep. These sarsen or sandstone boulders are the fragments of a former capping to the chalk in remote times. Palm trees grew from this, their roots causing holes in the stones. The sarsens were used by the megalithic builders of the Neolithic and Bronze Age periods. SOIL AND CULTIVATION: Chalk; unimproved downland. NEARBY LISTED SITES: Grey Wethers, The Polissoir, Devil's Den, Lockeridge Dene, Overton Hill, The Sanctuary. OTHER PLACES OF INTEREST, AND REFRESHMENTS: See under Silbury Hill.

Piggledene : the sarsen deposits once capped the chalk

The Polissoir Overton Down, north of West Overton, near Marlborough. Sheet 173, grid reference 128716, unmarked by the Ordnance Survey and unrecorded by the Victoria County History. Neolithic sarsen axe-grinding bench, 4000 to 2500 BC. ACCESS RIGHTS: None; it is on unimproved open downland about 150 yards from a right-of-way. *Lies to the north of the A4, five miles west of Marlborough. Park on the wide verge of the Ridgeway next to the Ridgeway Cafe car park. Walk north along the Ridgeway for a mile and a half to the gate into the Fyfield Down National Nature Reserve. This is signposted "Public Path, Ridgeway to Hackpen 4 ¼ , Chiseldon 10". Continue along the Ridgeway towards the skyline. As you approach the summit there is another Nature Conservancy brown information board at the far end of the reserve. Fifteen feet beyond it, also on the right of the track, is a metal gate. From it you see a scatter of sarsen stones in about 150 yards at the beginning of the gorse clumps. One prominent stone is triangular in outline and about four feet high. About 20 feet behind it is a large horizontal block of sarsen, about eight feet long and three feet wide, which is the stone in question.* ARCHAEOLOGY: This is a typical Polissoir of which many examples are to be found in France.

The Polissoir : sarsen stone worn smooth by axe grinding

There are only two in England, and this is by far the finer example. It was used by Neolithic man to sharpen his axeheads and arrows. There are six deep gashes in the south end of the stone, which represent use over a long period as sarsen is two-and-a-half times as hard as Aberdeen granite. The six grooves are between 18 and 24 inches long. At the side is a shallow recess or cuvette, smooth to touch, which served as a polisher or burnisher for the facets of the stone axe. This cuvette is about 12 inches long and an inch deep. The area beside it has also been polished smooth. Polissoir is merely the French word for polisher. SOIL AND CULTIVATION: Chalk; open downland studded with sarsens. NEARBY LISTED SITES: Grey Wethers, Piggledene, Devil's Den, Overton Hill, The Sanctuary, East

Kennett Long Barrow, Kennett Stone Avenue, Falkner's Circle, Avebury, Barbury Castle. OTHER PLACES OF INTEREST, AND REFRESHMENTS: See under Silbury Hill.

Ringsbury Camp Purton, near Swindon. Sheet 173, grid reference 075867. Iron Age hill-fort, about 50 BC. ACCESS RIGHTS: Five public paths converge on the fort. *Close to the B4041 between Purton and Wootton Bassett. Park in Restrop, the hamlet half a mile south of Purton. Pull on to the verge at the end of Bagbury Lane. Cross the main road and walk 40 yards to the tarred road opposite, to Restrop Farm. At the house you continue straight ahead along the side of the walled garden, into a sunken trackway. This tends to become a ditch, and if impassable follow it in the field. In a third of a mile it bends into the fort and the public path then runs along its outer bank.* ARCHAEOLOGY: Small but strongly defended double-banked fort enclosing about eight acres. The stout banks are constructed from limestone rubble. SOIL AND CULTIVATION: Limestone; southern bank overgrown, northern parts grassed. Interior has been ploughed but is now seeded back to grass. NEARBY LISTED SITE: Cricklade Saxon Walls. OTHER PLACES OF INTEREST, AND REFRESHMENTS: See under Cricklade Town Walls.

Ringsbury Camp : small but stoutly defended

Robin Hood's Ball Larkhill, near Amesbury. Sheet 184, grid reference 102460. Neolithic causewayed camp, 4000 to 3000 BC. ACCESS RIGHTS: Visible beside public right of way, but this is on the edge of the impact area of the Larkhill firing ranges and it is an offence to stray from the path, or to use it at all when the red flags are flying. *Turn north off the A344 on to the B3086 west of Stonehenge. Continue straight across at the next crossroads, passing Rollestone Camp. In just over a mile you come to a sharp corner after the Bustard Hotel. Park here and walk towards the corner, to the Bustard Verdette car park. Look at the flag pole beside the range office, and inquire if you are uncertain. It is only safe to proceed if no flag is hoisted. You can then walk around the back of the cottage opposite the Bustard Hotel, between the cottage garden and the coppice. Then follow the side of* *the wood, away from the Bustard buildings. You pass a "Warning to Public" notice about the danger of unexploded shells, telling you to keep strictly to public rights of way — which this is! The chalky track across wild downland leads in a straight line to the edge of Robin Hood's Ball, in just over half a mile. The causewayed camp lies between the path and an Ordnance Survey pillar, mainly to the right of this.* ARCHAE-OLOGY: Two irregular rings of bank and ditch enclose an oval space of two and a half acres, both ditches being broken by undisturbed causeways in the chalk. This is the oldest prehistoric site in the Stonehenge area and a fine example of a Neolithic camp — a stockade, settlement or even a burial area depending which archaeological report you read — of which about 30 have been found in the chalk and valley gravels of southern England. They probably served as tribal meeting places and ceremonial sites. Sherds of Windmill Hill type pottery have been found here in the ditches and below the outer bank. The reason for the romantic name is unknown. SOIL AND CULTIVATION: Chalk; open downland. NEARBY LISTED SITES: See under Stonehenge. OTHER PLACES OF INTEREST: Owing to the fact that the plain here is almost entirely under military rule there is very little of interest left to visit, and it is in any case a featureless and windswept landscape with few villages. REFRESHMENTS: Bustard Hotel, or return to Amesbury for a choice of good hotels and inns with bar food.

The Sanctuary Overton Hill, West Kennett, near Marlborough. Sheet 173, grid reference 118679. Late Neolithic timber buildings replaced by Early Bronze Age stone circles, 3000 to 2000 BC. ACCESS RIGHTS: In guardianship of the Department of the Environment, always open. *On south side of the A4, five miles west of Marlborough, opposite Ridgeway Cafe. Park on the north side of the road, on the wide verge of the Ridgeway next to the cafe car park. There is a gate into The Sanctuary on the other side of the road.* ARCHAEOLOGY: Concrete markers show the post holes of the Neolithic buildings. Six rings seem to represent three separate buildings from different dates. There is debate about whether it was roofed over. These posts were replaced by two concentric stone circles in the Beaker period of the Early Bronze Age, and linked with Avebury itself by the stone rows of the Kennett Avenue. John Aubrey's *Monumenta Britannica* shows the circles with 37 stones, 22 in the outer circle and 15 making up the inner ones. They were four to five feet high and most had fallen. The diameter of the outer circle was 130 feet. William Stukeley wrote that "this Overton Hill was until a few years ago crowned with a beautiful temple of the Druids and is still called The Sanctuary". All the stones were removed early in the 18th century but excavation in 1930 revealed their socket holes, and these are also marked by concrete pillars. An excellent key-plan with descriptive notes is set out on a metal plaque at the site. SOIL AND CULTIVATION: Chalk, grassland. NEARBY LISTED SITES: Overton Hill, Kennett Stone Avenue, Falkner's Circle, East Kennett Long Barrow, West Kennett Long Barrow, Silbury Hill, The Polissoir. OTHER PLACES OF INTEREST, AND REFRESHMENTS: See under Silbury Hill.

Scratchbury Hill Norton Bavant, near Warminster. Sheet 184, grid reference 913443. Iron Age hill-fort, about 50 BC. ACCESS RIGHTS: Public footpath along the top of the outer rampart on the northern side. Overlooks the A36 between Warminster and Heytesbury. Two miles east from Warminster there is a lane marked "North Farm" with a no through road sign,

The Sanctuary : before destruction, William Stukeley's 1723 drawing showing it at the end of the **Kennett Stone Avenue**, leading from Avebury, in a landscape dominated by **Silbury Hill**

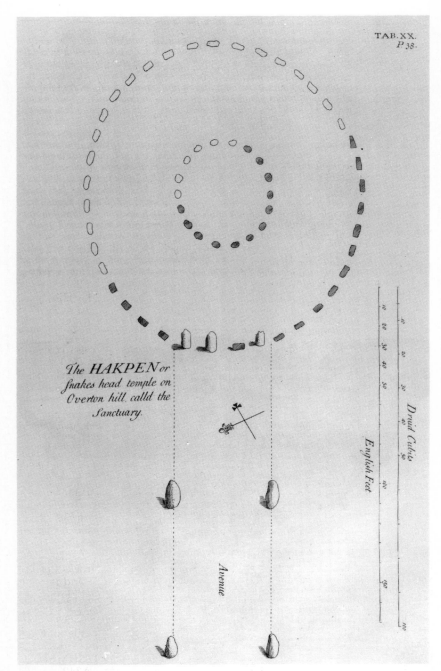

TAB. XX.
P 38.

The HAKPEN or
snakes head temple on
Overton hill, call'd the
Sanctuary.

Druid Cubits

English Feet

Avenue

The Sanctuary : Stukeley's plan of the stone circles

66

Scratchbury Hill : strongly defended by double banks

opposite a bus stop. Turn along it, over the railway line. In half a mile, after a cottage and at the top of the slope, you come to a sharp bend to the right. Park here, off the road at the corner, without blocking the gateway. Twenty yards from the corner, towards North Farm, there is a stile in the fence to your right. Follow the fence uphill to another stile and then walk up to the banks. The path, which is the Imber Ranges perimeter footpath, turns left along the rampart. ARCHAEOLOGY: Double banked fort with a ditch between, the earthworks strongly defending a huge area, 37 acres. Smaller inner earthworks pre-date the main fort. Delightful and superbly preserved, beneath a carpet of cowslips and harebells in spring, though there have been few archaeological finds, none of note apart from a bronze spoon discovered in 1804. SOIL AND CULTIVATION: Chalk; open downland. NEARBY LISTED SITES: Battlesbury Hill, Middle Hill, Cley Hill, Westbury White Horse, Bratton Castle. OTHER PLACES OF INTEREST: Heytesbury is a small town largely destroyed by fire some 150 years ago, but still with some fine old buildings. Norman arcades and chancel in the church, though it was rebuilt in 1867. Warminster is a military market town, seedy but interspersed with nice old homes. St Lawrence's church is 14th century. REFRESHMENTS: Red Lion and Angel Hotels at Heytesbury are recommended, and there is a wide choice in Warminster.

Sidbury Hill Tidworth Garrison, near Amesbury. Sheet 184, grid reference 216506. Iron Age hill-fort, about 150 BC. ACCESS RIGHTS: None, visible from public paths but not crossed by them. *West of the A338, north of Tidworth. This part of the army ranges is outside the impact zone and there is limited access. You are required to walk "only on public rights of way and on no account should any object be moved or touched. It may explode. Keep strictly to existing tracks". Look out for the "Tidworth Garrison" sign on the north edge of the base. Here, a quarter mile north of Tidworth Military Cemetery, in the dip, is a short stretch of old by-passed road, servicing two houses and a bungalow. The dirt track towards Sidbury starts from beside the bungalow drive and passes below the fort in about a mile. Sidbury Hill is conspicuous, being 735 feet high.* ARCHAEOLOGY: Double banked hill-fort enclosing 17 acres. Mutilation of the ramparts by tank tracks has revealed that the inner rampart was constructed in two periods, and the site has probably had a complex history. Views across the wild open downland of the Plain from tracks in this area are unsurpassed. SOIL AND CULTIVATION: Chalk; overgrown. NEARBY LISTED SITES: Casterley Camp, Gallows Barrow. OTHER PLACES OF INTEREST: Mediaeval castle at Ludgershall, opened to the public by the Environment Department. Pretty village and interesting church at Collingbourne Ducis. REFRESHMENTS: Good meals obtainable at the Crown Inn, Everleigh, on the A342.

67

Silbury Hill : view from Colt Hoare's *Ancient Wiltshire,* 1819 volume

Silbury Hill Avebury, near Marlborough. Sheet 173, grid reference 100685. Enigmatic prehistoric mound, its purpose unexplained, probably Early Bronze Age 2500 to 2000 BC. ACCESS RIGHTS: National Trust land, under the guardianship of the Department of the Environment and usually freely open, though at the time of writing it was closed to visitors due to excessive wear on the path to the summit. *Overlooks the A4, the Roman line of which deviated to avoid it, five miles west of Marlborough. There is a layby on the north side of the A4, between the road and the great ditch.* ARCHAEOLOGY: Conical mound, 130 feet high and 550 feet in diameter covering more than five acres. It is the largest man-made earth mound in Europe, though the lower quarter is natural chalk bedrock. It has all the appearance of an out-sized burial mound for some king but three excavations have failed to find a burial chamber. The first in 1777 by Cornish miners drove a shaft vertically from the summit to the original earth surface. The second in 1849 was made by Dean John Merewether, who tunnelled into the centre from a position inside the south ditch. This exploration again revealed no trace of a chamber. The latest expedition was in 1970 by Professor Richard Atkinson. This consisted of driving a slightly larger tunnel than the first into the

Silbury Hill : William Stukeley's engravings of the 1720s

69

Silbury Hill : surrounded by a great ditch

heart of the hill from a higher level and subsequently breaking into and following the 1849 tunnel to a point just beyond the centre of the hill. Once more no trace of a chamber was found, though the archaeologists expressed admiration for the skill of the prehistoric engineers and the way they layered the chalk to avoid slippage and achieved a stable angle of slope that is now 30 degrees. The purpose of Silbury remains a mystery but some archaeologists still believe it is a burial chamber, though this must lie outside the central area. Over the years it has produced odd finds of later date, such as a Viking bridle-bit that was in William Stukeley's collection. The great ditch has silted up and flooded like a moat, with a flock of swans on it, during the winter of 1981-82. SOIL AND CULTIVATION: Chalk; grassland. NEARBY LISTED SITES: West Kennett Long Barrow, Beckhampton Long Barrow, Beckhampton Roman Road, Avebury, Adam and Eve Stones, The Sanctuary, Overton Hill. OTHER PLACES OF INTEREST: The concentration of ancient monuments between Silbury Hill and Marlborough is overwhelming, and inescapable, though you can try Fyfield church, if only for its exterior and setting. Open country can be explored in the Nature Conservancy's Fyfield Down National Nature Reserve (see under Grey Wethers entry), for its rich downland flora and yet more ancient features, including a prehistoric field system. REFRESHMENTS: Reaching the sites scattered off the A4 between Silbury Hill and Marlborough entails plenty of walking, and there are simple meals and refreshments available at the Ridgeway Cafe, open all day throughout the year, opposite the Sanctuary at the top of Overton Hill. This is strategically placed at the centre of the longest walks, but take particular care if you turn right on leaving its car park and cut across both lanes of traffic — it is just over the brow of the hill and there is no visibility. Inside licensing hours there are excellent offerings at both ends of this valley, at the Wagon and Horses just east of the Beckhampton roundabout and the Red Lion in Avebury, and the group of inns and coffee shops at Marlborough.

Stock Bottom Roman Road Ford, near Salisbury. Sheet 184, grid reference 185332. Roman road, about 44 AD onwards. ACCESS RIGHTS: The Roman road is still a public right of way. *Beside the A30 two miles east of Bishopdown, Salisbury. At the top of the long hill there is a turn "Ford 1½" and a layby on this side road just below the "Ford" sign, 20 feet from the junction. The Roman road is on the opposite side of the main road, through a gate.* ARCHAEOLOGY: This is the best preserved length of the Wiltshire section of the Roman road from Salisbury to Winchester and London, one of the main arteries of Britain, for much longer than just the Roman period. Here it is about 20 feet wide and three feet high, though on the skyline it only shows in winter, as a flinty white line across the ploughed fields. SOIL AND CULTIVATION: Chalk; grass ploughed to edge. OTHER PLACES OF INTEREST, AND REFRESHMENTS: See under Figsbury Ring.

Stock Bottom Roman Road : preserved as a causeway in the foreground and visible as a chalky line in the distance

Stonehenge Amesbury, near Salisbury. Sheet 184, grid reference 123422. Neolithic henge monument of 2800 BC with Bronze Age stone circle, main structure erected between 2100 and 1900 BC. ACCESS RIGHTS: In guardianship of the Department of the Environment, visible from road and path, the public being allowed in 1982 to walk among the stones only on Tuesdays. *Just west of the junction of the A344 with the A303, two miles west of Amesbury roundabout. Has its own car park.* ARCHAEOLOGY: The name is mediaeval, meaning the "hanging stones". They are remarkable and unique, in that almost all are superbly carved, from boulders brought vast distances to this otherwise stoneless landscape. The great stones are sarsens from the Marlborough Downs, two and a half times as hard as Aberdeen granite, their present shapes — smooth tooled and squared with mortice and tenon joints — looking a world apart from their counterparts, the rough lumps known as the grey wethers on the downs above Marlborough. The earthen ceremonial avenue, along which the stones were dragged from the River Avon, is visible between Stonehenge and the Heelstone, the rough stone at the road. Basically Stonehenge is a vast religious centre and

the circle is only part of it. There are hundreds of round barrows in the vicinity and one can only assume their occupants wished to be buried in holy ground around the circle. The earliest structures of the circle were the bank and ditch, which is the Henge itself, the Heelstone and the Aubrey Holes all built about 2800 BC. After about seven centuries Stonehenge was radically remodelled. About 80 bluestones weighing up to about four tons were set up to form two circles, one inside the other, round the centre of the site. There was an entrance pointing towards the rising sun at midsummer. The bluestones came originally from the Preselly Mountains in South Wales. It seems that in period I there were two stones at the entrance with the Heelstone and a timber gate outside. In period II a double circle of bluestones (unfinished) and the Avenue were added. In period III sarsen stones replaced the bluestones and in period IV some of the bluestones were erected inside the circle. Finally in period V the bluestones were erected in a circle and a horseshoe. Some of the more recently noticed features of the monument are the daggers carved on the sarsens, the positions of which the guides can point out, which until a short time ago were linked with the Mediterranean world and regarded as evidence of foreign cultural influences. The re-calibration of radio carbon dating has made this supposition untenable and they must now be regarded as depictions of products from the home market. Though the main phase of Stonehenge is dated to the Bronze Age the stones still commanded respect in Iron Age and Roman times, there being no attempt to extend the Celtic field systems into the easily tilled area of the Plain surrounding the monument. Inevitably more detailed descriptions will be required and these are obtainable from the kiosk. The author strongly recommends ''Stonehenge and Neighbouring Monuments'' by Richard Atkinson (HMSO), ''The Enigma of Stonehenge'' by John Fowles (Jonathan Cape) and Rodney Legg's ''Stonehenge Antiquaries'' (Dorset Publishing Co.). SOIL AND CULTIVATION: Chalk; downland. NEARBY LISTED SITES: Cursus, Normanton Down, Winterbourne Stoke Roundabout, Woodhenge, Durrington Walls, Vespasian's Camp, Robin Hood's Ball. OTHER PLACES OF INTEREST: Salisbury with its magnificent cathedral and close is the earliest example of a mediaeval town that was deliberately planned, after the abandonment of Old Sarum. REFRESHMENTS: Ample at Salisbury and Amesbury and snacks, coffee and ice cream available at Stonehenge itself where the staff work hard and cheerfully to deal with the thousands of daily visitors from the four corners of the earth.

Stonehenge : the Office of Works restoration

Stonehenge : 'Slaughter' and 'Heel' Stones from the south-west during the 1920s restoration

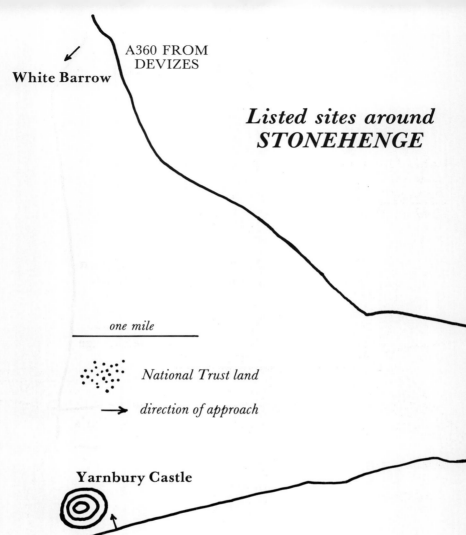

White Barrow

A360 FROM
DEVIZES

Listed sites around
STONEHENGE

_____ *one mile*

 National Trust land

⟶ *direction of approach*

Yarnbury Castle

A303 FROM
EXETER

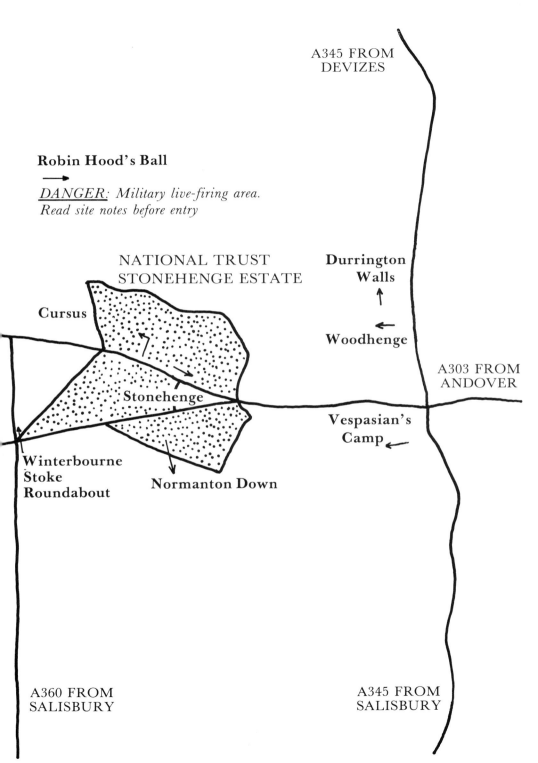

Swanborough Tump Manningford, near Pewsey. Sheet 173, grid reference 131601. Bronze Age burial mound, 2000 to 1500 BC, and Saxon meeting place, 850 AD. ACCESS RIGHTS: Shown on the map as being in the angle between a road and a public footpath, but read below. *North of the A345, turn off at Pewsey towards Woodborough. It is midway between Pewsey and Woodborough, on the south side of the road beside the wood opposite the entrance to Cocklebury Farm. This is two miles from the A345 at Pewsey. A public footpath runs between it and the wood.* ARCHAEOLOGY: A plaque opposite the farm road reads: "Swinbeorg, circa 850. Meeting place of the hundred of Swanborough." As "Swana beorh" it is reputed to be the meeting place of a Saxon hundred court where Ethelred and Alfred the Great held a state council. But what has happened to the Bronze Age round barrow on which they met? There is something of a small mound in the trees behind the plaque, but the map shows it in the corner of the field. Here it was recorded in the 1950s as a mound 60 feet in diameter by three feet high. There is nothing remarkable in that, but the site is now a flat field. It was a scheduled ancient monument and typifies the fate of hundreds of smaller antiquities in Wiltshire that went under the plough in the post-war farming revolution. SOIL AND CULTIVATION: Sandy, ploughed and under cereals. NEARBY LISTED SITES: Adam's Grave, Knap Hill. OTHER PLACES OF INTEREST: Statue of King Alfred at the southern village part of Pewsey, where the group of streets face a low bridge over the infant Avon river. REFRESHMENTS: Inns at Wilcot and Woodborough.

Three Shire Stones Collerne, near Corsham. Ordnance Survey sheet 172, grid reference 796700. Late Neolithic burial chamber, 3500 to 2500 BC. ACCESS RIGHTS: On the verge of the highway. *Beside the Fosse Way, two*

Three Shire Stones : reconstructed burial chamber

thirds of a mile south of the main runway of Collerne Airfield. On the roadside edge of corner of park wall, beside a line of beech trees. ARCHAEOLOGY: Fanciful reconstruction of 1736, with three large blocks of oolitic limestone, six feet high, supporting a capstone eight feet by four feet by two feet thick. These were from a burial chamber of an otherwise disappeared long barrow. Known as Three Shire Stones as this was the meeting place of the historic boundaries of Wiltshire, Gloucestershire and Somerset. SOIL AND CULTIVATION: Limestone; amongst trees. NEARBY LISTED SITES: Lugbury, Lanhill Long Barrow. OTHER PLACES OF INTEREST, AND REFRESHMENTS: See under Lanhill Long Barrow.

Tidcombe Down Long Barrow Tidcombe, near Hungerford. Sheet 174, grid reference 293576. Neolithic chambered long barrow, about 3500 to 2500 BC. ACCESS RIGHTS: Beside a road, with a public path close to its east side. *Turn off the A338 between East Grafton and Shalbourne, on to the tarred line of the Roman road over the downs above Tidcombe, which becomes the Chute Causeway. The barrow is on the north side of this road on the spur of the hill half a mile south of Tidcombe.* ARCHAEOLOGY: A mound 180 feet long by 60 feet wide which is orientated only slightly eastwards of north to south. Four sarsens are exposed at the southern end, about ten feet high, and the whole mound has been torn apart. In contrast to the pillage by the gentry that went under the name of barrow digging, the sack of the Tidcombe Long Barrow was carried out by the proletariat. It was done by the villagers in 1750, though their search for treasure yielded only one skeleton. SOIL AND CULTIVATION: Chalk; grass. NEARBY LISTED SITE: Fosbury Camp. OTHER PLACES OF INTEREST: Pumping station from reservoir at Wilton beside the canal on the other side of the A338, to the chain of a dozen locks upwater from Little Bedwyn. This is the active section of the Kennet and Avon Canal. REFRESHMENTS: Inns at Burbage and Shalbourne.

Upper Upham Settlements and Fields Aldbourne, near Hungerford. Sheet 174, grid reference 230770. Bronze Age, Iron Age and Roman settlements and fields, probably continuously occupied from 1500 BC to 450 AD. ACCESS RIGHTS: Public byway passes through the centre of the field system. *Above the A419, Hungerford to Swindon road, two miles on the Swindon side of Aldbourne at Aldbourne Warren Farm there is a tarred road westwards from the brow of the hill signed: "Public right of way to Upham". On the sides and the top of the downs there are hundreds of acres of ancient field banks, either side of the road.* ARCHAEOLOGY: Remarkable for its extent, continuity, state of preservation — one of the last major blocks of unploughed downland in these parts — and the richness of the many finds. These have existed in quantity over the years, even though most of the land is undisturbed open sheep-range, turning up in molehills and rabbit warrens. Many were Iron Age brooches from an extensive settlement. These native field systems continued into Roman times but may have been brought into the estate system in the late 3rd or during the 4th century. This development was also substantial, the lead pipes of "a range of Roman baths" being found in the 1880s. Coins, pottery, bracelets, and spearheads have been uncovered. It is an area where future discoveries may be expected, and perhaps even a site of national importance. SOIL AND CULTIVATION: Chalk with some scattered sarsen stones; open downland. NEARBY LISTED SITES: Aldbourne Four Barrows, Membury Fort, Littlecote Roman Mosaic, Liddington Long Bar-

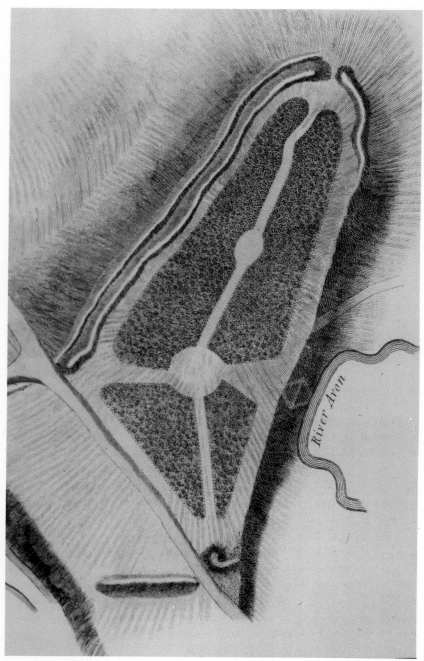

Vespasian's Camp : plan from Sir Richard Colt Hoare's *Ancient Wiltshire,* 1812 volume

row. OTHER PLACES OF INTEREST, AND REFRESHMENTS: See under Aldbourne Four Barrows.

Upton Great Barrow Upton Lovell, near Warminster. Sheet 184, grid reference 955423. Bronze Age round barrow, about 2100 to 1900 BC. ACCESS RIGHTS: In the angle between two public rights of way. *Approached from the A36, Warminster to Salisbury road, at Upton folly. The track up to the barrow is immediately opposite the turn to "Upton Lovell". It is a mile walk, to the wood at the top of the hill, and the barrow is immediately to the right of the track where it forks.* ARCHAEOLOGY: Important classic site, a bell barrow 175 feet across by ten feet high which had a bank outside its ditch. A necklace from the mound, of amber, shale and faience beads, is in Devizes Museum. Another nearby barrow, since destroyed, was known as the "Golden Barrow" for its treasure of gold plate, 1,000 amber beads (worth more, in weight, than gold) grape-shaped cup, drum-shaped gold beads and gold-coated shale button. SOIL AND CULTIVATION: Chalk; wooded. NEARBY LISTED SITES: Codford Circle, Yarnbury Castle. OTHER PLACES OF INTEREST, AND REFRESHMENTS: See under Scratchbury Hill.

Vespasian's Camp Amesbury. Sheet 184, grid reference 146417. Iron Age hill-fort, from about 150 BC. ACCESS RIGHTS: Visible from road, but not crossed by any public path, so permission to walk on the banks must be requested at West Amesbury Farm. *Turn off the A345 into Amesbury town centre, and continue west through the town until you reach open country. Here there is a layby on the north side of the road about 100 yards after the army gates beyond the last house. The road is in a cutting at the junction and Vespasian's Camp stands above it, the banks overlooking the "Lake, Woodford" road sign.* ARCHAEOLOGY: Large single-banked fort with a second counterscarp rampart which gives the appearance of double-banking, enclosing 37 acres. Its name, associating it with the Roman conqueror of Wessex, is of some antiquity, being current before John Aubrey's time. SOIL AND CULTIVATION: Chalk; wooded with tall beeches along the length of the bank. NEARBY LISTED SITES: See under Stonehenge. OTHER PLACES OF INTEREST: Amesbury is a small market town now much under army influence. The church, closed in winter, was built by the Saxons and refashioned by the Normans. It is very beautiful. There was also an abbey church, but no trace of it remains. REFRESHMENTS: The Antrobus Arms Hotel at Amesbury provides good meals, and accommodation for those needing a base from which to explore the archaeology of the Plain.

Wansdyke Wiltshire section, above Vale of Pewsey from Morgan's Hill to Savernake Forest. Sheet 173, grid reference 023672 and then eastwards. Dark Ages frontier defences, about 550 AD. ACCESS RIGHTS: Though in places there are gates to climb, particularly in a farm owned by the Crown estates after Shepherds' Shore on the Devizes road, making it difficult to know quite what is the course of the path, you can be assured that public rights-of-way stretch on or beside the entire length of the bank from Morgan's Hill eastwards to the tree-covered length of bank that descends to opposite Shaw House on the road from Lockeridge to Alton Barnes — a distance of nearly ten miles. The rest of the route to Savernake Forest is cut about by ploughed land and only partly incorporated into the footpath network. *Take the A361 from Devizes towards the Beckhampton roundabout and turn*

Wansd.

Wansdyke : surmounted by a gibbet on Morgan's Hill, drawn by William Stukeley in 1724

Wansdyke : its course over Tanhill, the 964 foot peak of these downs with a view that takes in the Black Mountains of Wales and the spire at Salisbury

Wansdyke : the frontier against the Dark Ages, at Morgan's Hill, from Colt Hoare's *Ancient Wiltshire,* 1819 volume

Wansdyke : descends tree-covered to Shaw House

west towards Calne, to the north of the Bishops Cannings signs, two miles north of Devizes Barracks. Park in two miles, at the hilltop picnic area just after the golf course. A track leads on to higher ground, bringing you on to the Wansdyke on Morgan's Hill, at the point where it branches off from the Bath-London Roman road. From here it runs on to the higher downs, to the right of the masts, as a great bank with a deep ditch to the north of it, unbroken for miles. The walk is truly magnificent but it is best attempted in spring or autumn since it is very tough, with no shade and long grass to wade through. On the right day it is one of the loveliest walks in England. ARCHAEOLOGY: This great earthen defence, originally palisaded, was probably constructed by the Romanised Britons after the decay of the empire in the mid-6th century AD. It was designed to hold back the pagan Saxon onrush, and in this it was successful as no pagan Saxon burials have been found south of this dyke. At its highest point the Wansdyke runs across the northern edge of Tan Hill, formerly known as St Anne's Hill, which used to be the site of a sheep fair. From its 964 foot peak you can spot the steeple of Salisbury Cathedral, and look westwards to the Black Mountains in Gwent. SOIL AND CULTIVATION: Chalk; mainly open downland, eastern section partly overgrown with scrub and trees. NEARBY LISTED SITES: Beckhampton Roman Road, Adam's Grave, Knap Hill, Lockeridge Dene. OTHER PLACES OF INTEREST: Bishops Cannings is a charming village with one of the loveliest of 12th century churches. Note the queer old almsbox with three locks set on a post, and the curious old chair with its gloomy latin tags. This may well be a pre-Reformation confessional. Look up at the gargoyles all round the church, and note the old Mass dial on the wall. Devizes is the best centre for exploring this area, and do not fail to visit the museum of the Wiltshire Archaeological and Natural History Society in Long Street. It is one of the finest regional collections in the country, with much that has come from the sites that make up these listings. This material is of international fame. Devizes is a small market town with 16th century timbered houses clustering around the church. REFRESHMENTS: Ample refreshments and accommodation in Devizes, where the Bear Hotel was the birthplace of Sir Thomas Lawrence, the great painter.

West Kennett Long Barrow West Kennett, near Marlborough. Sheet 173, grid reference 104677. Late Neolithic chambered long barrow, about 3500 to 2500 BC. ACCESS RIGHTS: In guardianship of Department of the Environment, always open. *Five miles west of Marlborough, on south side of the A4. Park in the layby just to the west of a thatched cottage, opposite the sign "West Kennett Long Barrow 1m". The path crosses a stream and then is double fenced to the top of the hill.* ARCHAEOLOGY: One of the biggest long barrows in Britain,

West Kennett Long Barrow : spectacular tomb

but the claim on its information board — that it is the largest long barrow in England and Wales — is exaggerated. Nearby East Kennett is a little larger in terms of area, and much bigger in cubic capacity. But West Kennett is spectacular as a wedge-shaped mound 340 feet long by 75 feet wide with a line of great blocking stones at the east end. The largest of these is a huge central stone 12 feet high. On more than one of the uprights there are polished grooves caused by the sharpening of stone axes. Behind these stones lies a passage of sarsen boulders with drystone walling, partly corbelled at the top and eight feet high, stretching 40 feet into the mound. It has two pairs of side chambers. Current archaeological thought is that these, to quote Colin Renfrew, represent "the realisation in stone of the wooden mortuary chamber of the earthen long barrow". A couple of glass bricks in the roof provide a reasonable amount of light, but it is more fun if you bring the torch from your car. This was dug into by Dr Robert Toope in the 17th century to provide bones for medicine-making. The eastern chamber — now open to the sky — and 15 feet of the passage were cleared by John Thurnam, a surgeon who collected and studied skulls, in 1859. In 1955 Stuart Piggott and Richard Atkinson excavated the remaining four chambers, finding some 20 burials. The associated pottery and flints, and some bone objects, showed the burials extended over a thousand years, from 3500 to 2500 BC. Nearly all the adults suffered from arthritis and several from spina bifida. When the tomb was eventually closed it con-

The Long Barrow S. of Silbury Hill.

West Kennett Long Barrow : its unrestored appearance, drawn by William Stukeley

tained about 50 burials. Exhibits from the mound are in the British Museum and Devizes Museum. Originally the barrow had side ditches that were ten feet deep, but these do not now show under the ploughed land at the edge of the mound. SOIL AND CULTIVATION: Chalk; the mound is unploughed downland. NEARBY LISTED SITES: Silbury Hill, The Sanctuary, Kennett Stone Avenue, Falkner's Circle, Avebury, Adam and Eve Stones, Beckhampton Long Barrow, East Kennett Long Barrow. OTHER PLACES OF INTEREST, AND REFRESHMENTS: See under Silbury Hill.

Westbury White Horse Bratton, near Westbury. Sheet 184, grid reference 898516. Hill-figure, its predecessor possibly Iron Age about 50 BC. ACCESS RIGHTS: In guardianship of the Environment Department, always open. A mile and a half west from Westbury, above the B3098. *Turn off uphill to Bratton Castle, three miles east of Westbury at the west end of Bratton village. Parking area at the far side of the hill-fort. Follow the outer bank towards the valley, where it turns the corner. The White Horse is down the steep, 50 degree slope.*

ARCHAEOLOGY: Oldest and most interesting of the Wiltshire white horses. Even in its present state it dates from 1778 and is earlier than the others, but there was an even older white horse beside or under it. Shown in the 1772 edition of "Britannia" as being originally long and thin like the Celtic lines of the Iron Age Uffington White Horse of the Berkshire Downs. It had a crescent-tipped tail typical of the shapes on Celtic coinage. Traditionally, however, it was said to have been cut by Alfred the Great to celebrate his crucial victory over the Danes at Edington in 878 after a battle lasting nine days. The surviving Danes fled to Bratton Castle hill-fort where they held out for a further week. As a result of this battle the Danish king Guthrum and his chiefs were baptised Christians. Whatever its origins, the responsibility for sweeping away the genuine horse and making its replacement rests with a land steward of appropriate name, a Mr Gee. SOIL AND CULTIVATION: Chalk; downland escarpment. NEARBY LISTED SITES: Bratton Castle, Battlesbury Hill, Middle Hill, Scratchbury Hill. OTHER PLACES OF INTEREST: Bratton church should on no account be missed as it is one of the finest in Wiltshire, being an outstanding example of early perpendicular work at its best. Edington has the most perfect surviving monastic church in the county. The remains of the priory of the Bonhomme monks are around the old grey house with the crenellated frontage north of the graveyard. The priory was founded by William of Edington at the request of the Black Prince. Westbury is a quiet market town with a magnificent church but little else of importance. REFRESHMENTS: Ample at Westbury and Warminster.

White Barrow Tilshead, Salisbury Plain. Sheet 184, grid reference 033468. Neolithic earthen long barrow, about 4000 to 3500 BC. ACCESS RIGHTS: National Trust land, always open. *Park half a mile south of Tilshead, beside the A360 by the Tilshead village sign. This is opposite the junction to "West-down Camp". A trackway beside the barns is signposted "Public Footpath Chitterne 3½". The barrow is on the skyline in a third of a mile. As you approach it you see a "Private Lane Keep Out" sign, which is aimed at the army rather than the public. There is a stile into the National Trust compound which protects the barrow and a clump of trees from the surrounding army lands.* ARCHAEOLOGY: One of the best preserved long barrow burial mounds in Wiltshire, orientated east to west. It is 255 feet long by 155 feet wide at the nine feet high eastern end. Wide side ditches are perfectly preserved, four feet deep. Sectioned by Colt Hoare, inconclusively. A layer of black earth was found, possibly showing the site of a decayed wooden mortuary chamber, and some antler picks. Name "Whitebergh" in use in 1348. SOIL AND CULTIVATION: Chalk; open downland. NEARBY LISTED SITES: Robin Hood's Ball, Yarnbury Castle. OTHER PLACES OF INTEREST: There are plentiful ancient features, but most tend to be within the impact areas of the army ranges, though the public trackway beside the White Barrow continues southwards for four miles to Yarnbury Castle. REFRESHMENTS: The inn at Tilshead, or in Shrewton.

White Barrow : magnificently preserved

White Sheet Hill (Ansty) Ansty, near Shaftesbury. Sheet 184, grid reference 943242. Neolithic long barrow, about 4000 to 3000 BC, and late Roman ditches, about 450 AD. ACCESS RIGHTS: Beside public right of way. *Look out for the Donhead St Andrew and Berwick St John turn-offs from the A30, five miles east of Shaftesbury, and continue about half a mile eastward from them. White Sheet Hill is the end of the great escarpment to the south of the main road, with a wide entrance to an old quarry at its foot. Park here, opposite the house. Walk up the steep and rutted trackway to the summit. The long barrow is about 150 yards along the flat land at the top, on the left above a small spruce planting.* ARCHAEOLOGY: The long barrow is about 135 feet long and seven feet high, its sides flanked by well-marked side ditches that are four feet deep. The hill has a complicated later history. There is a ditch between two banks of great height, known locally as "Half Mile Ditch". The larger bank is on the western side and it seems probable that this unusually formidable defence was thrown up by the Romanised Britons as a barrier against Saxon infiltration. NEARBY LISTED SITES: Winklebury Hill, Castle Ditches. OTHER PLACES OF INTEREST: Opposite the barrow, 100 yards away on the Shaftesbury side,

White Sheet Hill (Ansty) : the long barrow

there is a reminder in the corner of the field of when this track was the Great Western Post Road from London to Exeter, a milestone inscribed "XCVII (97) miles from Hyde Park Corner XIV (14) from Salisbury 1736". Alvediston churchyard, in a superb setting, has the grave of Sir Anthony Eden, Britain's Suez period Prime Minister. He spent his declining years in the house a few yards down the lane. REFRESHMENTS: Excellent meals and snacks in the 16th century inn at Alvediston, the Crown.

White Sheet Hill (Mere) Mere, near Shaftesbury. Sheet 183, grid reference 803347. Neolithic causewayed camp, 4000 to 2500 BC, Bronze Age barrows about 1800 BC and Iron Age hill-fort, about 150 BC. ACCESS RIGHTS: The Neolithic camp is owned by the National Trust, who also own the northern half of the hill-fort. *Take the B3095 northward from the A303 at Mere, towards Kingston Deverill, up the steep hill on to the downs. Half a mile after the top you come to a drove road that crosses the tarred road. Park here and walk along the left-hand track, westward, for about a mile. The track then runs into National Trust land, acquired in 1982 as an extension of their Stourhead estate. The hill-fort is to the left and the much slighter circle of the causewayed camp lies 500 yards north of it, crossed by the track just before it bends to the left.* ARCHAEOLOGY: The causewayed camp encloses about five acres and is one of the stockades or ritual circles of the first farmers. Professor Stuart Piggott found Windmill Hill type pottery in the silting of the ditch. But the big fort to the south is the obvious archaeological feature, triple banked on the side you approach but with only one rampart needed above the steep escarpment. About 15 acres

White Sheet Hill (Mere) : Iron Age banks

are enclosed. The circular earthwork within is probably a mediaeval beacon. Unexcavated, but probably built in two or three phases. There are also a dozen Bronze Age barrows scattered over White Sheet Hill, which is scarred as well by five ancient cross-ridge dykes and a set of strip lynchets. Quite apart from all this there are Celtic fields, nine pillow mounds — rectangular, enclosed by ditches, possibly rabbit warrens — an undated enclosure, the pale of a mediaeval deer park, two 18th century milestones, and some quarries. It is one of the finest examples of multi-period field archaeology anywhere in Britain. SOIL AND CULTIVATION: Chalk; open downland. NEARBY LISTED SITES: Cold Kitchen Hill, Cley Hill. OTHER PLACES OF INTEREST: The hill overlooks the National Trust flagship estate of Stourhead, given to the nation by Sir Henry Hoare in 1947. His ancestors included the 19th century Wiltshire antiquary Sir Richard Colt-Hoare, and their house is open daily except Fridays from May to September. The outstanding 18th century gardens, perhaps the most famous in England, are open daily throughout the year. In Mere, near the church, is a Tudor house, the Chantry, where William Barnes the poet kept school for some years. Woodlands Manor just south of the town is a very early home, of the time of Chaucer, and should not be missed if it is open. REFRESHMENTS: The Old Ship and Talbot Hotel at Mere serve very good snacks, and in the Stourhead environs there is the public house beside the lower car park and the Red Lion Inn at Kilmington, the next village.

Wick Ball Camp Dinton, near Wilton. Sheet 184, grid reference 000320. Iron Age hill-fort, about 250 BC. ACCESS RIGHTS: Eastern rampart on National Trust land and listed in their handbook ''Properties of the National Trust'', a fact you may need to know as we were intercepted in the park. *Dinton is on the B3089, which joins the A30 at Barford St Martin. Drive along St Mary's Road to the north end of the village. The entrance to Dinton Park is to the north of the church. Although you may find closed signs these refer to the house, which is leased to the YWCA. The park, however, is freely open. Walk up the drive and beside the house. The track swings to the right after the back entrance, uphill. After about 30 yards there is a wooded ride, leading off on the left to an orchard. Towards the end of the orchard, opposite the gate to the walled garden, is a flight of steps called Jacob's Ladder. At the top, the track to the left leads to Wick Ball Camp, about 150 yards into the wood. It is however on the limits of the National Trust land, and permission for a proper exploration has to be arranged with the adjoining farmer, Mr Webb of Teffont.* ARCHAEOLOGY: A small but stoutly defended Iron Age fort, with a single ditch and high rampart, enclosing seven acres. Unfortunately the camp is much neglected and overgrown, though the setting is splendid on a sunny day. SOIL AND CULTIVATION: Greensand; wooded. NEARBY LISTED SITES: Hamshill Ditches, Chiselbury Camp. OTHER PLACES OF INTEREST: Philipps House, which you pass, is open to the public on Wednesday afternoons only, April to September. Built in 1814 by William Wyndham, in Chilmark stone. Given to the Trust in 1943 by the Philipps family, and now a conference centre. Dinton also has the birthplace of Edward Hyde, Earl of Clarendon, who played such a large part in sorting out the aftermath of the Civil War and wrote the standard work on ''The History of the Great Rebellion''. The Teffont villages are extremely beautiful with delightful groupings of cottages around the stream. REFRESHMENTS: The Black Horse at Teffont Magna provides good bar snacks and meals.

Windmill Hill Avebury, near Marlborough. Sheet 173, grid reference 086714. Neolithic causewayed camp, about 4000 to 2500 BC, with later Bronze Age round barrows, 2500 to 1500 BC. ACCESS RIGHTS: National Trust land in the guardianship of the Department of the Environment, freely open. *Turn off the A36 midway between Avebury and the Beckhampton round-about, northward to the hamlet of Avebury Trusloe. You pass a small housing estate and go straight over at a crossroads, following the Windmill Hill signs. Continue until you reach a sign that says the track is not suitable for motors and proceed from here on foot, until you reach a gate on the right with a signpost to Windmill Hill.* ARCHAEOLOGY: The classic type-site for its period, with a large 20 acre enclosure encircling a rounded hilltop, dug by early farmers who had migrated from northern France. There are three concentric rings. A dwarf was buried in the newly dug outer ditch, possibly as a foundation sacrifice. There were other human bones excavated by Alexander Keiller from 1924 to 1929. He also found the remains of cattle, goats, sheep, pigs and dogs as well as leaf arrowheads and polished flint axes and some imported axes. The potsherds proved to be of secondary Neolithic cultures, with sherds of A and B1-classified beakers. These, and antler combs and saucer-shaped grain rubbers are on display in the museum at Avebury. Quantities of hazel-nuts and the remains of crab apples suggested seasonal human activity, possibly linked with the rounding up and stockading of cattle in the autumn for the reduction and dispersal of herds. Several barrows were built on the hilltop during the Bronze Age, after the enclosures had been abandoned, and urns and grave-goods from these are in Devizes Museum. The large one, known as Picket Barrow, is a bell-shaped mound eighty feet in diameter and eight feet high. One of the smaller mounds was dug before 1849 and yielded a grape cup — shaped like a round cluster of grapes — and a perforated battleaxe from Cwm Mawr in Shropshire. SOIL AND CULTIVATION: Chalk; previously half was under the plough but it is now restored to grass. NEARBY LISTED SITES: Avebury, Adam and Eve Stones, Beckhampton Long Barrow. OTHER PLACES OF INTEREST, AND REFRESHMENTS: See under Avebury.

Winterbourne Stoke Roundabout Stonehenge, near Amesbury. Sheet 184, grid reference 101416. Neolithic long barrow, about 4000 to 3000 BC, and Bronze Age burial cemetery, 2100 to 1500 BC. ACCESS RIGHTS: Visible from the A360 north from the roundabout at what was formerly known as Longbarrow Crossroads. *The roundabout is on the A303 a mile and a half west from Stonehenge. Layby on the north side of the road 300 yards on the Stonehenge side of the roundabout, beside a beech wood.* ARCHAEOLOGY: Major Stonehenge-period group of circular burial mounds, which can now be considered about the best preserved in Britain — since post-war ploughing reduced those at nearby Normanton to patches of undergrowth in the barleylands. The earliest of the mounds beside the roundabout, a long barrow, is superb. It is about 250 feet long and 10 feet high, with flanking quarry ditches. Apparently it covered one male skeleton, which was unusual under-use for this communal type of grave. The later round barrows were for single burials. These barrows are also magnificent, still on grassland and grazed in a way that enables their subtle shapes to be understood. We should not forget that graves of all periods were made to be tended, and the complex Wessex types are only understandable when they are preserved under close-cropped turf. They stretch out in a line following the north-

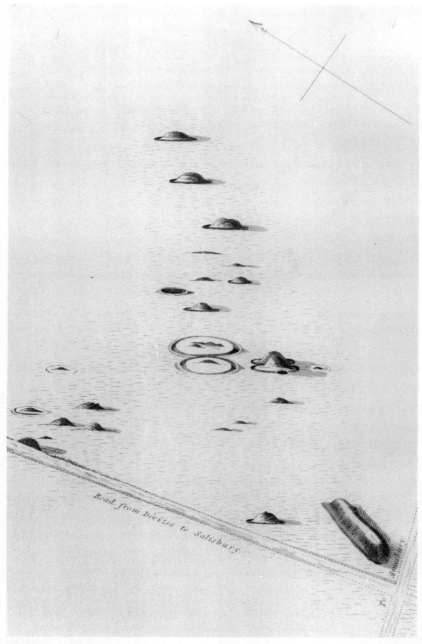

Within the image: *Road from Devizes to Salisbury*, *To Amesbury*, *To*

Winterbourne Stoke Roundabout : the roundabout now being at the bottom right, showing the variety of barrow types. From Colt Hoare's *Ancient Wiltshire*, 1812

Winterbourne Stoke Roundabout : superb long barrow

easterly alignment of the earlier long barrow. Bell barrows, disc barrows, saucer barrows, and even the rare pond barrows — in reverse to the rest, as a circular depression rather than a mound — all are here. Grave goods in Devizes Museum include daggers, beads, incense cups, a stone macehead, grape-shaped cup and beaver teeth. SOIL AND CULTIVATION: Chalk; grassland. NEARBY LISTED SITES, PLACES OF INTEREST, REFRESH-MENTS: See under Stonehenge.

Winkelbury Hill Berwick St John, near Shaftesbury. Sheet 184, grid reference 952217. Unfinished Iron Age hill-fort, about 43 AD. ACCESS RIGHTS: Beside a public bridleway, but not crossed by it so permission to walk on the hill should be requested at the farm. *Berwick St John is south from the A30, turn off five miles east of Shaftesbury. Proceed through Berwick St John and drive out of the village on the Alvediston road. There are a few houses by the village sign, and a layby. Beyond the left-hand cottage there is a trackway with a bridleway sign to "Higher Bridmore 1½". It is a deeply cut sunken lane smothered in wild garlic in summer. Half way up, the main track bends to the right and becomes much*

Winkelbury Hill : unfinished hill-fort

91

deeper. The fort is at the top of the bank to the right. ARCHAEOLOGY: Important in that it was built in a hurry and never finished, perhaps being started when the first news came of the Roman invasion. An older existing settlement, from about 200 BC, is scattered across the hill, with traces of pits and huts. The proposed line of the late Belgic hill-fort encloses 12 acres, the only properly constructed section being a long high bank along the south side. Even here there is a big gap, marking the proposed site of the entrance gates and outworks. SOIL AND CULTIVATION: Chalk; open downland. NEARBY LISTED SITES: White Sheet Hill at Ansty, Castle Ditches. OTHER PLACES OF INTEREST: Berwick St John is a small but beautiful village with an interesting church. REFRESHMENTS: Obtainable from the inn at Berwick St John, or southwards at the King John Inn, Tollard Royal.

Woodhenge Amesbury. Sheet 184, grid reference 151434. Neolithic timber temple, about 3000 to 2500 BC. ACCESS RIGHTS: In guardianship of the Environment Department, freely open. *Turn west off the A345 at the signpost to "Woodhenge" just beyond the Amesbury sign at the north end of the town, by the last street light. Woodhenge is in 200 yards, on the left opposite the tourist information office. The entrance is just round the corner.* ARCHAEOLOGY: Wood-

Woodhenge : ditch and post-holes showed from the air in the 1920s

henge, known then as Dough Cover, was thought to be a flattened disc barrow until Squadron Leader Insall spotted a series of circular white marks in the ploughed soil in 1925 and took aerial photographs. The position of these post-holes is now marked with circular concrete blocks. Surrounding them is a low circular bank which had an internal flat-bottom ditch originally eight feet deep. There was a causewayed entrance on the north-east side. Inside are six concentric oval rings of holes which held the

Woodhenge : the post-holes are now marked by rings of concrete pillars

wooden posts. The long axis points to the rising sun on midsummer day. There are larger post holes (red on plan at the site) which do not form part of any of the rings. These had sloping ramps cut into the chalk, down into which the post had been slid when they were erected. Once the posts were upright the holes and ramps were filled with rammed chalk. Near the centre was a grave containing the body of a three-year-old child whose skull had been deliberately split. Its site is marked with a hump of flints. This was probably a dedication burial and is one of the few cases that indicate human sacrifice in Neolithic Britain. The posts could have stood in the open, painted and carved, or they might have been the uprights of a roofed building. As the largest posts are in the third ring such a building would probably have looked like a huge thatched barn bent around on itself leaving an open space in the centre. Four other poles were set beyond the circle as sighting posts for sunrise at the summer solstice, like the Heelstone at Stonehenge. This suggests that Woodhenge was a prototype for Stonehenge. Whatever its form it was probably a temple or tribal meeting place. SOIL AND CULTIVATION: Chalk; grassland. NEARBY LISTED SITES, PLACES OF INTEREST, REFRESHMENTS: See under Stonehenge.

Wudu-Burh "Camp of the Wood" (now known as the "Roman Village") Knighton Hill, Broad Chalke, near Wilton. Sheet 184, grid reference 058238. Iron Age and Romano-British settlement, from about 150 BC to 450 AD. ACCESS RIGHTS: Beside public footpath but ask permission at the farm to explore the earthworks. *Approach from the A354, Blandford to Salisbury road, leaving it at the dual carriageway. Take the Broad Chalke turn. In a mile or so, at the top of the hill, there is a trackway opposite a wood. Beside it are old army buildings and a house. This is the Ox Drove, signposted to Lodge Farm. After the farm you continue along the track for a further mile, to the tarred road to Knighton Wood Farm. Here you turn left, northwards, along the tarred road for about half a mile. The "Roman Village", as the farmhands call it, is in the dry valley immediately before and to the right of the plantation.* ARCHAEOLOGY: Major Iron Age and Romano-British settlement in a beautiful setting at 500 feet, its field surviving as a relic of ancient downland amongst the new barleylands. The settlement incorporated cattle and sheep penning. Excavation revealed abundant pottery from the Early Iron Age to the end of the Roman period. A coin of Marcus Aurelius (161 to 180 AD) was recently found there. As a location, the gamekeeper observed to us, it is always warm and drains well. SOIL AND CULTIVATION: Chalk; unimproved downland listed by the Nature

Wudu-Burh : the 'Roman Village' as the locals call it

Conservancy as a site of special scientific interest, for cowslips, orchids and rich flora, cherished by its owner who forbids any use of fertilizers on the land, and has an excellent pheasant-shoot in compensation. NEARBY LISTED SITES: Chiselbury Camp, Castle Ditches, Grim's Ditch, Ackling Dyke. OTHER PLACES OF INTEREST: Fine and unspoilt churches at Bishopstone and Stratford Tony. REFRESHMENTS: The White Hart at Bishopstone does excellent bar meals.

Yarnbury Castle Wylye, near Wilton. Sheet 184, grid reference 036403. Iron Age plateau-fort, first fortified about 280 BC, present form about 25 BC. ACCESS RIGHTS: Beside and visible from public trackways, though not actually crossed by them. *On the north side of the A303 at the top of the long hill eastward from the spaghetti junction at Wylye. Large layby on the Exeter-bound carriageway, on the brow of the hill above Wylye. Cross the main road, walking along the greensward between the carriageways. On the other side, in about 300 yards at the top of the hill, there is a farm track into the earthwork. A quarter of a mile after this is another trackway which skirts the east side.* ARCHAEOLOGY: The finest hill-fort in Wiltshire. It is not often realised by those who marvel at such great hill-forts as Eggardon or Maiden Castle that infinitely more expenditure of labour is required to throw up banks if only half the size upon a level plain as at Yarnbury, which encloses 29 acres. It is one of the largest and best preserved of the plateau camps. Being on a plain the ramparts look higher than they really are — the highest point is only 25 feet though Hoare, Allcroft and Cox all gave the height as over 50 feet! These earthworks were set out for slingstone warfare, calculations of the range of this weapon at differing elevations being necessary to determine precise distances between

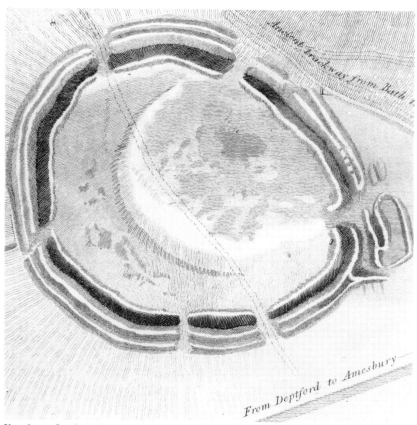

Yarnbury Castle : plan from Sir Richard Colt Hoare's *Ancient Wiltshire*, 1812 volume

the banks. The aim was to keep the advantage with the defender. An attacker on, say, the middle bank would be just within range of the defenders on the inner bank, but the difference in elevation between the banks would prevent the attacker from returning the fire. There are six entrances into the fort but only one, that on the eastern side, can be considered original. This is provided with outworks of bastion-like proportions to guard the gates and the innermost ditch is distinctly recurved inwards at the entrance. The other gaps in the defences doubtless came about because for many generations a large sheep fair was held here on 4 October each year until 1916. The side of the fair lies within the central ring, and probably is the original encampment of the early Iron Age. The ditch of this earthwork is five feet deep. Other internal features, such as the outlines of pennings, date from the sheep fairs. SOIL AND CULTIVATION: Chalk; downland. NEARBY LISTED SITES: Codford Circle, Upton Great Barrow, and for those to the east see under Stonehenge. OTHER PLACES OF INTEREST: Winterbourne Stoke looks dreary from the A303 but if you walk down Church Street it becomes very pretty. The early Victorian vicarage is a classic example of its type, and the church of St Peter is early 12th century.

Yarnbury Castle : entrance defended by outworks

Berwick St James, on the B3083, is a charming little village with a church built in 1116. Stapleford, where there is a Mass dial in the church porch, is also well worth a short stroll. REFRESHMENTS: Bell Inn at Winterbourne Stoke, the Boot Inn, Berwick St James. Good food available at the Pelican Inn, Stapleford, which also offers accommodation and is an ideal point for the exploration of eastern Wiltshire.

Books consulted

Abury. William Stukeley, 1743
Ancient Earthworks of Cranborne Chase. Heywood Sumner, 1917
Ancient Wiltshire. Sir Richard Colt Hoare, 1812-19
Archaeology of Wessex. L.V. Grinsell, 1958
Avebury Monuments. Environment Department guide, HMSO 1976
Before Civilisation. Colin Renfrew, 1976
Excavations in Cranborne Chase. Lieut. Gen. Augustus Pitt-Rivers, 1887
Guide to Prehistoric England. Nicholas Thomas, 1960
Highways and Byways in Wiltshire. N. Erickson, 1917
A History of Wiltshire. Volume One, Part One. Oxford, 1957
Monumenta Britannica. John Aubrey. Dorset Publishing Co., 1980-82
Stonehenge and its Monuments. Richard Atkinson, HMSO, regularly reprinted
Stonehenge Antiquaries. Rodney Legg, editor. Dorset Publishing Co., 1982
Wessex from the Air. O.G.S. Crawford, 1928

Other specialist reports were loaned by the archaeological booksellers Fox and Co., 30 Princes Street, Yeovil, Somerset. Antiquarian works provided by the Wimborne Bookshop, 26 West Street, Wimborne, Dorset.